JOCKS AND NERDS

Men's Style in the Twentieth Century

Richard Martin
Harold Koda

RIZZOLI
NEW YORK

First published in the United States of America in 1989 by
RIZZOLI INTERNATIONAL PUBLICATIONS, INC.
597 Fifth Avenue, New York 10017

Copyright © 1989 Rizzoli, New York

Library of Congress Catalog Card Number 88-43418
ISBN 0-8478-1045-3
ISBN 0-8478-1046-1 (pbk.)

Designed by Charles Davey
Composition by David E. Seham Associates,
Metuchen, New Jersey
Printed and bound by Toppan Printing Company,
Tokyo, Japan

PAGE ONE: Suspenders featured in a fashion editorial,
published in *Esquire*, New York, March 1988.
Photographer: Marcia Lippman

FRONTISPIECE: Mixed Metaphors. Ensembles by
Franco Moschino. Fashion editorial published in
Mondo Uomo, Milan, January 1988. Photographer:
Tony Thorimbert. Courtesy Edizioni Edimoda S.p.A.

THESE PAGES: Two men in sportswear on the beach.
1987. Photographer: Tom McBride. Courtesy the
photographer

CONTENTS

INTRODUCTION

Jocks and Nerds is neither a sociological treatise nor a fashion manual. Instead it is a proposition about the way men dress in the twentieth century. We believe that men are knowing in making choices among style options, and that they dress to create or recreate social roles. Both men and women seek to realize roles and identities, but since men's options in dress would appear to be the more acutely restricted, perhaps selecting a role has assumed more importance for them than it has for women. A man's role is his operative identity; style choices follow therefrom. He may see himself as a sportsman and thus may affect the garb of the country gentleman. His role is subject, however, to the evaluation of others; the sportsman may be avatar to the game hunter and anathema to the animal lover. His clothing may cry out his identity—and if he elects to wear a Norfolk jacket with belted back or plus fours and argyles, his choices may strike others as alluring or inane.

These varying interpretations of a role provide the subjective element in male attire. Late in a century when male dress has been increasingly stabilized and even codified, we are still partisan and personal in our evaluation of clothing and style. For some, clothing from a given store may be burnished with aristocratic valor, but for others it may lack idiosyncrasy or temperament. Too, perceptions of roles vary with the times: when the Establishment is in the ascendant, the role of the businessman may be preferred; in other social climates, more self-expressive roles may be esteemed. A military hero in one era may be reduced to histrionic patriot in another. And the rebel may be perceived as socially advanced or society's pariah.

Twelve male identities have been proposed for *Jocks and Nerds*. The choices are most decidedly arbitrary, yet they represent twelve persistent style modes of the twentieth century. We have tried to see them in terms of their cultural and stylistic continuity throughout the century and to put in perspective the meaning of the clothing selected by the wearer in his projection of a role. The roles selected are the Jock, Nerd, Worker, Rebel, Cowboy, Military Man, Sportsman, Hunter, Joe College, Businessman, Man about Town, and Dandy. The Jock and Nerd have been granted star billing because they are roles that have arisen to new respectability in the present day. It is not our intention to divide all men into one category or the other—although the temptation to do so is there. The Jock is the health nut, the fitness addict, the man who participates fully in the game(s) of life. The Nerd is the egghead, the intellectual, the outsider plucked from the limbo to which he was confined by the 1950s. He has stature and status—and his clothes have been emulated by a new generation of bespectacled, white-socks-and-black-shoes wearers.

There are a number of reasons for these choices. Tradition has long been honored in men's fashion, but in the past decade the classics have been forcefully reinterpreted as never before. Although it is unlikely that more than a few men will again sanction plus fours and argyle socks for their sporting attire, their intense devotion to the tweed jacket and the country look testifies that the golfing and hunting traditions have not been deserted by the contemporary male. Calvin Klein has given new wing to the aviator jacket; Ralph Lauren has signed the polo shirt

contemporary fashion image
er French man of letters
héophile Gautier (1811–1872) as-
bes romance to the clothing of
e past and to the man who wears
ntemporary clothing in recogni-
n of historic styles.

*POSITE: Ensemble by Mila Schon
mo; tie by Prochownick. Fashion edi-
ial published in* Uomo Harper's Ba-
*r, Milan, March–April 1988. Pho-
rapher: Nick Scott. Courtesy Edizioni
ds-Italia s.r.l.*

th options of contemporary colors; Giorgio Armani has scouted the
American West and taken captive the duster; and Jean-Paul Gaultier
has redefined the motorcycle jacket.

Despite its earthbound gravity, men's clothing aspires to magical
transformations. Men's fashion magazines of the 1980s can be read as
quest literature pursuing historical ideals. Writers' styles are "quoted"
as if prose might be surpassed by fashion. To be like a famous author,
to live in a world of another time and place, to achieve the success of
others by dressing similarly, these are all attractive prospects offered
in fashion magazines to men today. All that is necromancy and alchemy
in this potent exchange with another life or an earlier time is, in some
quarters, made science by the doctrinaire writings of those who promise
personal and professional success through correct appearance.

Society's sanctions through etiquette and authority's through ad-
vancement can seem to be powerful endorsements for a given role. But
the scientific formulas for success seldom allow for the pleasure of
adopting several roles, the fulfillment of personality through dress, or
the possibility of a personal decision. Would a businessman care to walk
in the shoes of James Joyce? In the intimacy of a clothing decision, he
might, signaling an affinity with the writer. Such specific identifications
are fostered by advertisements and editorial coverage in menswear
magazines and reinforced by designers' style names; the male chooses
a family tree, a heritage, a sense of identity or likeness that is most
compelling because it is not enunciated but simply visually implied.

In metaphor and in reality, there are seven ages of man. But his style
of dress tends to originate in adolescence. Thus many aspects of male
dress are an extension of roles from high school and college. Even
"jock" and "nerd" bespeak the epithets and heroes of a time when men
are allowed their first options in dress. Joe College may pass through
many ages still wearing the same college tie and, if not the same blazer
and loafers, then others in never-ending succession. All the while he
remains unyieldingly fixed to the campus, even as he grows older, until
at last he can enjoy the college reunions for which he has always been
appropriately dressed. Joe College never ages and never varies. His lapels may alter by an inch or two and letter sweaters may be more or
less available, but few such sartorial traditions vanish altogether.

The conservatism and consistency of men's clothing give it continuing availability. For women, fashion is an ineluctable force. The same
style of clothing is rarely available from one season to the next, either
from a single store or from a manufacturer. Men's clothing is more sta-
ble; classic models remain ever present. To be free from capricious
fashion change does not mean, however, that men do not make
thoughtful decisions about their attire. On the contrary: because fashion does not prevail, choices become even more important. For example, the man who wears a bow tie may conform to every announced
convention, but he will never be elected President and may never make
a corporate chief executive. Yet the man who wears French cuffs may
be either a maître d'hôtel or a powerful leader, but he is also a man of
style. The color of a man's socks may classify him as a renegade, a daffy,
or a conservative; to wear no socks at all is the privilege of the contemporary upper class. Because men's style is so tradition-bound, any decision, no matter how subtle, transforms the role and the man.

As individual and self-defining as these decisions may be, men's style
choices are also collectively made. When Clark Gable took off his shirt
in It Happened One Night (1934), his bare chest was revealed and undershirt sales plummeted. When Indiana Jones in Raiders of the Lost Ark
(1981) became the adventurer of choice for millions of moviegoers,
Stetson hats enjoyed a short-lived revival. Not only idols and daredevils
but also the elegant Edwardians of television's "Brideshead Revisited"
(1981) and film's Chariots of Fire (1981) held brief sway, leading men to
emulate the stars and become those roles as if actors themselves, putting
on costume to achieve the parts of protagonists and heroes. Conventional wisdom has it that men dress to be conventional, but those with
insight into male dress might hold that men dress to realize dreams, to
fulfill themselves through being someone other than themselves. If, as
Shakespeare would have it, "apparel oft proclaims the man," perhaps
it is true that it both claims and proclaims him.

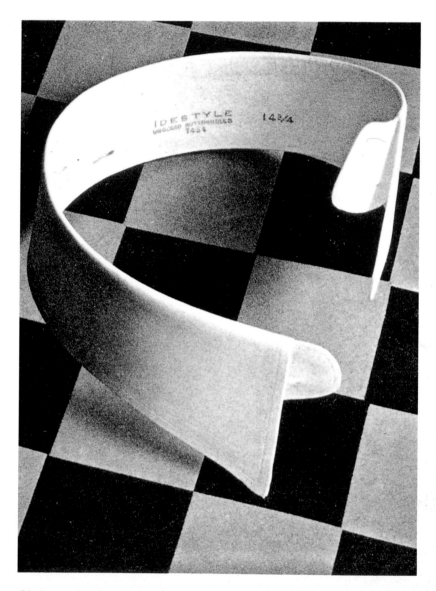

Clothes make the man, according
to the aphorism; indeed, they have
the iconic potential to describe the
man, even in his absence. An oarsman's "civies" hanging in an emp-
ty locker room provide a telling
portrait of the businessman at leisure. The noted photographer Paul
Outerbridge, Jr., creating a study
in modernist abstraction, nonetheless represented modern man.

OPPOSITE: Locker room of the Vesper Boat
Club, Philadelphia. Published in M, New
York, January 4, 1984. Photographer:
Dan Coxe. Courtesy Fairchild Syndica-
tion. ABOVE: Collar. 1922. Photogra-
pher: Paul Outerbridge, Jr. Collection The
Museum of Modern Art, gift of the pho-
tographer.

At left, fashion casts James Joyce in "A Portrait of an Artist as Men's Style." Although Joyce played with the unconscious in his novels, he affected an academic conservatism in his dress. In these fashion images, the orthodox is combined with touches of the idiosyncratic dandy, and aspects of the bespectacled artist's own visage are conflated with those of his imaginary characters, Stephen Dedalus and Buck Mulligan. The figure in the dressing gown perhaps alludes to Mulligan, whose comic celebration of the rites of shaving at the opening of *Ulysses* was conducted in such attire.

After James Joyce. TOP LEFT: Paisley-printed silk robe and shirt by Stefano Ricci; tie by Krizia; glasses by Allison. BOTTOM LEFT: Suit and shirt by Alberto Zanre; coat by Brooksfield; bow tie by Pal Zileri for Forall; glasses by Allison. Fashion editorial published in Uomo Harper's Bazaar, *Milan, January–February 1988. Photographer: Nick Scott. Courtesy Edizioni Syds-Italia s.r.l.*

...ernational literary figures from ... nineteenth and twentieth cen-...ics provide types for contempo-... male dress. Faintly renegade ...character, yet evocative of hero-...minds, the images encourage the ...n to take poetic license in ...aking with the conventions of ...siness dress and to allow person-...tyle, sanctioned by history and ...ers, to prevail.

OPPOSITE TOP: After Federico Garcia Lorca. Jacket and shirt by Guy Laroche; tie by Prochownick. OPPOSITE BOTTOM: After Walt Whitman. Ensemble by Ungaro Uomo; hat by Borsalino. Photographer: Romano Grozic. TOP LEFT: After Ralph Waldo Emerson. Ensemble by Gianni Versace. Photographer: Peter Gravelle. BOTTOM LEFT: After F. Scott Fitzgerald. Suit by Antonio Baldan; shirt by Dajana; tie by Erreuno; handkerchief by Stefano Ricci. Photographer: Romano Grozic. TOP RIGHT: After Eugene O'Neill. Blouson by Breco's; polo shirt by Ocean Star; trousers by Missoni Uomo. Photographer: Romano Grozic. BOTTOM RIGHT: After Henry Miller. Ensemble by Gian

Paolo Orani; tie by Canasta; hat by Borsalino; glasses by Silhouette. Photographer: Peter Zander. All from fashion editorial published in Uomo Harper's Bazaar, Milan, March–April 1988. Courtesy Edizioni Syds-Italia s.r.l.

alian designer Franco Moschino,
modern-day Daumier, caricatures
cial roles in his advanced cloth-
g of the 1980s.

EFT: Prep meets punk. *RIGHT: The*
tablishment meets Rambo. Ensembles
Moschino. Fashion editorial published
Mondo Uomo, Milan, January
88. Photographer: Tony Thorimbert.
urtesy Edizioni Edimoda S.p.A.

Advertising images have long represented models for men. The cool charm of the Hathaway Man has sold shirts for more than thirty years, as did that of the Arrow Collar Man, created by illustrator J. C. Leyendecker, before him. Advertising imagery for men, often romantic in inspiration, makes that romance accessible by association with the products it seeks to sell.

OPPOSITE: The Hathaway Man: "How to keep Cool when Terrified." 1958. Advertisement. Photographer: Paul Radki. Courtesy International Museum of Photography at George Eastman House.

Movies have played an important role in the creation of male imagery in the twentieth century. Like Clark Gable in *It Happened One Night* (1934), men have found that they, too, can dispense with an undershirt. The casual elegance of Fred Astaire, whose relaxed rehearsal clothes set styles as readily as did his formal, white-tie-and-tails dance clothing, has been emulated by men of fashion since the early 1930s. Some thirty years later, a generation of young men would seize on the style of Warren Beatty's costumes for *Bonnie and Clyde* (1967). An appropriate antihero for the decade, bank robber Clyde Barrow was depicted wearing suits with the respectability and tradition to get him into banks as well as the insouciant flair to get him out with the deposits.

TOP RIGHT: Warren Beatty in Bonnie and Clyde. *1967. Unknown photographer for Warner Bros. Courtesy Kobal Collection. CENTER: Clark Gable and Claudette Colbert in* It Happened One Night. *1934. Unknown photographer for Columbia Pictures. Courtesy Kobal Collection. BOTTOM RIGHT: Fred Astaire in rehearsal. 1934. Unknown photographer for RKO. Courtesy Kobal Collection.*

In the movie *Chariots of Fire* (1981), immaculate sporting looks of the 1920s, redolent with class associations, were examined in a manner that established the decade's preoccupation with historicism in clothing. Lord Snowdon's elegant photographs inspired by the film suggest the conspiracy of photography, film, and marketing to create style for men.

After the film Chariots of Fire, *1981. RIGHT: Oxford Bags–Cleaverly Pants by Alan Flusser. OPPOSITE: Sweater by Cesarani. Advertising campaign for Bloomingdale's, New York. 1982. Photographer: Lord Snowdon. Courtesy Bloomingdale's and the photographer.*

Ian Charleson of "Chariots of Fire."
Photographed by Snowdon.

Ben Cross of "Chariots of Fire" photographed by Snowdon.

C E S A R A N I   1 9 8 2

The Classic Cricket Sweater (And National Pastimes)

The Cricket Sweater—Cricket players turned to the ease of sweaters by the early 1900's. White reigned the field and team colors were marked by stripes or the color of a cap. Eventually, the cricket sweater left the field and became a fashion item.

Here, Cesarani's pure cotton cricket sweater thickly knit in the traditional cable-stitch. Now, a neat continental alternative for everyday, everywhere. Remaining the same over so many years because its final form was perfect.

On 1, New York. And in all our fashion stores.

bloomingdale's men's store

The Cricket Sweater: White with maroon/yellow/navy stripes, navy w/maroon/yellow/white or yellow w/green/navy/maroon. For sizes S.M.L.XL. 65.00. An easy, offhand casual that doubles for the game of business day-to-day, or when you're up at bat this weekend. And just the right touch of warmth (and pure classic style) to welcome the first brisk air of spring. Also, **The Natural Straw Boater**, 45.00.

The television series "Brideshead Revisited" (1981) also had a dramatic impact on men's clothing in the 1980s, confirming and extending the 1920s revival of *Chariots of Fire*. The attention to the attire of young Sebastian Flyte and Charles Ryder at Oxford seemed to confirm the fine tailoring of English aristocratic dress. It sent men back to English tailors and to American designers such as Alan Flusser, who represent the British heritage.

ABOVE: Anthony Andrews and Jeremy Irons in the television series "Brideshead Revisited." 1981. Unknown photographer for Granada. Courtesy Kobal Collection.

Fashion magazines have also cast noted artists and actors in the role of style leaders.

LEFT: David Hockney and Jack Nicholson with their fashion doubles. Fashion editorial published in GQ, New York, *June 1987. Courtesy Condé Nast Publications, Inc.*

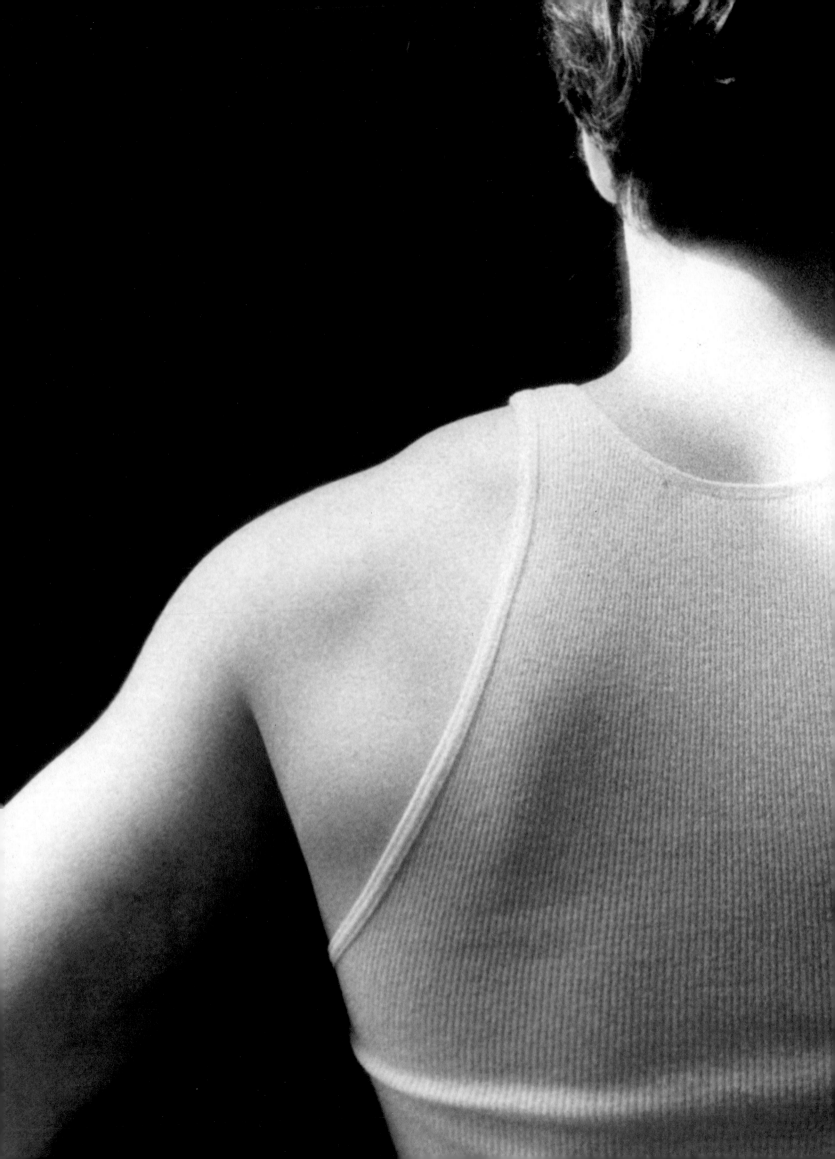

The jock ideal arises from the traditional notion of the sound body. In a century when leisure has theoretically become available to men of all classes, the physical ideal has been extended as much to fitness as to the pleasures of sports and competition.

PRECEDING PAGE: Jock in tank top. 1983. Photographer: Marcia Lippman. Courtesy the photographer. RIGHT: Gymnastics. Photomural by Leo Lances. 1939. WPA Community and Health Building at the New York World's Fair. Courtesy National Archives.

Johnny Weissmuller, gold-medal swimmer at the Olympic Games of 1924 and 1928, poses before the official poster of the Los Angeles Olympics of 1932. That same year, Weissmuller was starring in his first Tarzan movie, the apotheosis of the jock as primitive hero.

LEFT: Johnny Weissmuller. 1932. Unknown photographer. Courtesy Kobal Collection.

To be the embodiment of physical prowess is the traditional ideal of t
athlete. He aspires to heroic achievement on the playing field
whether that be the neighborhood sandlot, the college football stadiu
or the international field of competition at the Olympics. From the fi
Panhellenic games of 776 B.C. to the Olympiads of the present day, t
athlete has been revered not only as the paragon of physical develo
ment (implying beauty) but also as the civic symbol. His achieveme
has been tested in competition, and his victory has cast reflected gle
on the community.

Now the victorious athlete, a beau ideal for any people, would se
impervious to criticism. But the young athlete in his prime, who h
submitted himself to a regimen so obsessive that his muscles have d
veloped at the expense of his intellect, is often called a jock. The te
came into widespread use on college campuses in the 1950s, wh
football players were none too affectionately referred to as "jockstrap
a reference to the athletic supporters they were known to wear. A d
cade later, in 1965, the champion free-style swimmer Don Schollanc
(winner of gold medals in four events at the 1964 Olympic Gam
would enter college at Yale, where, he said, "my classmates expect
me to be a jock, inarticulate, unintelligent, and interested only
sports." In the intervening years, however, the appellation has be
used more affectionately as interest in health and fitness has grown a
the professional athlete has become so well compensated that the i
tion of the "dumb jock" has been rendered irrelevant.

Although campus and community have both created jock hero
perhaps the national hero is the most compelling. Johnny Weissmull
swimming champion in the 1924 and 1928 Olympic Games, was su
a figure; he would transfer this heroism to film, as, in 1932, he beca
the first of several athletes who starred as Tarzan. Like the athlete
Greek Classical sculpture, he was the man undressed. In a society u
comfortable with the naked man, the exposure of the male body
sanctioned and aesthetically perfected only through art. Athleti
however, also provides the rare exception of the male revealed.

Clothing for the jock is the necessary attire for the sport—and
more. Weissmuller may be dressed for a swim-suit advertisement as
poses before the 1932 Los Angeles Olympics poster (he did not compe
in that year), although his spear would also suggest that he is posing
the Tarzan role. Some forty years later, in 1972, Mark Spitz, also a go
medal-winning Olympic hero, became a popular idol, here wearing t
official bathing trunks of the American Olympic team. In this case, J
Palmer, for thirteen years an outstanding pitcher for the Baltimo
Orioles (and a multiple winner of baseball's Cy Young Award), is
vested of the team uniform as he advertises a brand of men's underw
(somewhat slyly styled "Jockey"), which also provides an excuse
the locker-room deshabille of sports. Indeed the classification of me
underwear into "jockey" and "boxer" shorts, both alluding to spor
seems to imply that the sanction of athletics is required for manly attire

Vigor and athletic prowess may be suggested by wearing spo
clothes. In 1920, the Prince of Wales (the future Duke of Windsor) d

eissmuller, dressed in a robe em-
zoned with the Olympics insig-
a, poses for celebrity portrait
otographer Nickolas Muray,
rhaps on the return voyage from
e 1928 games in Holland. Mark
itz, winner of seven gold med-
s in swimming at the 1972 Olym-
s, wears the Stars and Stripes of
e American team's uniform.
ke other Olympic heroes, both
en made the transition from

sports to entertainment, Weissmuller in movies, Spitz, for a time,
in television.

*OPPOSITE TOP: Johnny Weissmuller.
c. 1928. Photographer: Nickolas Muray.
Courtesy International Museum of Photography at George Eastman House.
OPPOSITE BOTTOM: Mark Spitz. Published in* Life, *New York, September 15,
1972. Photographer: John Zimmerman.
Courtesy Time Inc.*

Edward, Prince of Wales, is the
British sportsman as jock. The
tank top has been worn by athletes
since the beginning of the century
but never with greater elan than by
the Prince of Wales, in 1920. In
contrast, baseball hero Jim Palmer,
in 1988, poses in near nudity, modeling the men's underwear called
"Jockey" shorts. Palmer is a true
sports star, having won the prestigious Cy Young award in 1973,
1975, and 1976 and having been
the youngest player ever to pitch a
World Series shutout. In this advertisement, his endorsement and
his physique are called upon to sell
underwear.

*TOP: Edward, Prince of Wales. 1920.
Unknown photographer. Courtesy Li-
brary of Congress. BOTTOM: Athlete Jim
Palmer for Jockey underwear. 1988. Ad-
vertisement. Unknown photographer.
Courtesy Jockey International Inc.*

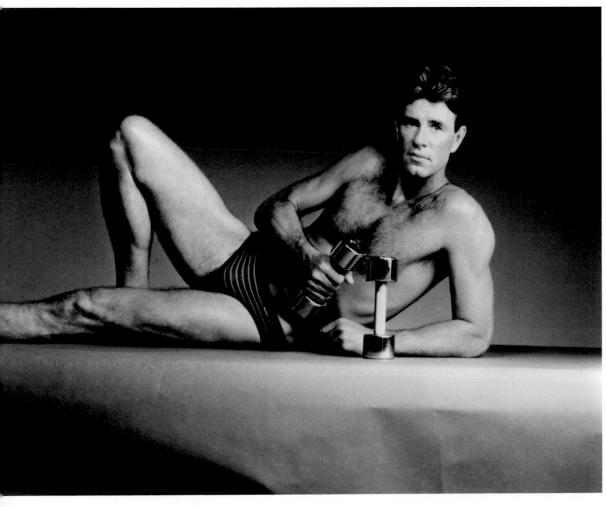

Actors Sylvester Stallone, opposite, and Dolph Lundgren, below, wear boxing trunks that might be considered regulation. In the nineteenth century, pugilists customarily wore skintight knit trunks, but in the early years of the twentieth century, the great boxer Jack Johnson so intimidated his opponents when appearing in tight shorts that baggy trunks became standard dress for boxers.

Boxer shorts, identified with the physicality of the ring, assume a shapeless awkwardness when revealed as underwear.

LEFT: David McDermott in college. c. 1973. Photographer: Josef Astor. Courtesy the photographer.

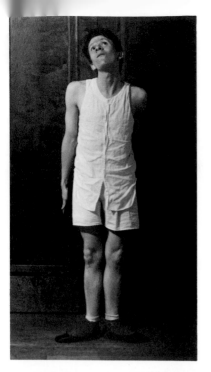

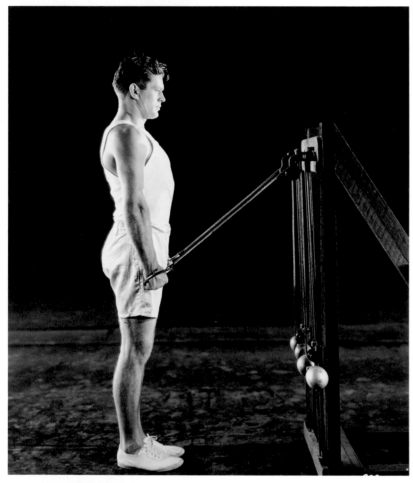

Gene Tunney, world heavyweight boxing champion from 1926 to 1928, and Ramon Novarro, the Mexican actor whose best-known silent film was *Ben Hur* (1925), wear similar costumes for their workouts. The tank top, initially functioning as swimwear, was adopted for gymnastics and track. It surpassed its original function in the 1970s, when covert clothing came out into the open and was adapted for street garb.

ABOVE: Gene Tunney exercising. c. 1927. Unknown photographer. Courtesy Library of Congress. LEFT: Ramon Novarro. 1929. Photographer: C. S. Bull for MGM. Courtesy Kobal Collection.

plays physical readiness if not ruggedness in the oarsman's tank top; in 1925, actor Ramon Novarro, not known as an athlete, emulates oarsman and wears his clothes. In the 1980s, as the regimen of sp expanded through the widespread founding of health and exerc clubs, prime physical conditioning became the preserve not just of young but of men of any age. Sophisticated Nautilus and Soliflex chines replaced the simple apparatus for exercising demonstrated Gene Tunney in 1927. At the same time, sports attire seemed to p from the health club to everyday life. Tank tops, gym shorts, jogg shoes, sweatshirts, and other accoutrements of the jock were be worn on the street. In this era of body awareness and concern for phys prowess, there emerged mythic heroes—"superjocks"—personif on film by Sylvester Stallone, in whom heroism is nearly overwhelm by narcissism.

Although the modern Olympic athlete enjoys the simulation of ancient palaestra for his deeds, the sandlot must suffice for the ordin jock. The clothes of the athlete are appropriated with a dashing urba by the New York messenger, who wears the sweatband and rac shorts derived from competitive cycling. The cycle messengers b upon the scene in the 1980s, adopting the Spandex, knee-length sh worn by competitors in the Tour de France. Blithely moving across c barriers, the middle-class devotees of exercise quickly appropriated style, identifying with the energy and physical accomplishment pressed in both sports and commerce.

The mesh shirt, a light training shirt that supplanted the cotton je in football, is another example of a sports usage entering the vocabu of casual clothing. Made of inexpensive, easily cleaned, man-mad bers, it has, as viewed by photographer Marcia Lippman on the W Point cadets, a numinously artificial, otherworldly look that ingeniou mimicks nature's honeycomb. The mesh shirt is expressive of functional needs of the athlete, akin to shoulder padding and cl cropped hair. But the same shirt passed quickly from gridiron to str in the 1980s.

Athletic gear has been appropriated for street use by such dive figures as Elvis Presley and Andy Warhol, who wore their sneakers away from the realm of sports. Sweat suits, initially the exercise clot of young athletes warming up for football, basketball, and other te sports, are now worn with equal aplomb by a no-sweat President, str wise kids, and fashion followers with only the most modest variati in the attire. The baseball jacket and cap and training shirts and sh are eligible for continuous wear in a society that celebrates the athl male. The canniest and best designers in both Europe and Ame have fully grasped the merits of active sportswear and assimilated forms and values into high style. The Duke of Wellington said the tle of Waterloo was won on the playing fields of Eton (where the Eng public school boy learned to play for blood), and today's sports cloth has won its share of competitions, as well. The clothing of the athl heroic by dint of its functionalism, takes part in the largest gam modern life—leisure activity.

If the archetype of the athlete is the witless team player, more phys than mental or spiritual, his antagonist might seem to be the eggh intellectual. Yet, in the modern era, they can dress in the same wa robe, enjoying the widespread acceptance of active sports and sw clothing and the notion that every man is a relative equation of m and body, expressed in clothing.

In 1987, Woody Hochswender, a fashion writer for *The New York Times,* called New York's bicycle messengers "envoys of chic." One young man, top left, wears an artfully tied kerchief as sweatband, in preference to the more functional athletic version in terrycloth. The European bicycle racer's costume, involving skintight nylon pants, emigrated to America early in the decade and was taken up by the "winged Mercuries" swiftly negotiating New York's busy streets. Quickly adopted by fashion, above right, and by the leisured middle class, bottom left, the pocketless, tightfitting pants were frequently worn with a strapped-on nylon pouch for carrying necessities. The bicycle pants represent a sleek moment in the 1980s when manmade materials were permitted to replace the usual preference for natural fibers.

TOP LEFT: *Man with sweatband. 1981. Photographer: Andre Grossman. Courtesy Staley-Wise Gallery.* BOTTOM LEFT: *Bicyclist in racing shorts. 1987. Photographer: Tom McBride. Courtesy the photographer.* ABOVE RIGHT: *Man in cycling shorts by Paulo Gabini; turtleneck by Jockey; waistcoat by Tommy Nutter. Fashion editorial published in* The Face, *London, June 1985. Photographers: Ray Petrie and Jamie Morgan. Courtesy Buffalo, London.*

The striped rugby shirt, top and bottom, customarily worn in the English version of football, has become recreational wear in America with colors no longer specific to a team. Since rugby is seldom seen in this country, the special allure of this garment may have been its English origin rather than its connection with the popular spectator sport.

TOP: Man in rugby shirt. c.1982. Photographer: Joan Liftin. Courtesy Archive Pictures Inc. BOTTOM: Man in rugby shirt. 1987. Photographer: Tom McBride. Courtesy the photographer.

The American game of football, opposite, in its physical contact and roughness perhaps the quintessential jock sport, has provided its own contributions to active sportswear. In the 1980s, the typical cotton football jersey gave way to the mesh shirt, and what was new on the playing field within a few seasons became new attire for the street.

OPPOSITE TOP AND BOTTOM: West Point football team. 1987. Photographer: Marcia Lippman. Courtesy the photographer.

The pairing of outerwear with sweat pants in the 1980s followe[d] tendency to incorporate lowly at[h-] letic gear into the most vernacul[ar] improvised dress. As if in fulfill- ment of a prophecy published in DNR, in December 1978—"Ma[y-] be we'll get to the point where t[he] President of the United States will wear a pin-striped, vested warm-up suit"—in 1984 Preside[nt] Ronald Reagan appeared before reporters on Air Force One wear[ing] sweat pants, collar, and tie.

OPPOSITE TOP: East Boston yout[h,] hooded sweat shirt. 1985. Photograp[h:] Rosewell Angier. Courtesy Archive [Pic-] tures Inc. OPPOSITE TOP, INSET: Ma[n,] T-shirt and sweat pants by Spirito; ja[cket] by Sicons. Fashion editorial publishe[d in] L'Uomo Vogue, Milan, January 19[.] Photographer: Claus Wickrath. Cou[rtesy] Edizioni Condé Nast S.p.A. OPPOS[ITE] BOTTOM: Man in sweat pants, [and] leather jacket by Claude Montana. F[ash-] ion editorial published in Vo[gue] Hommes, Paris, September 1983. [Pho-] tographer: François Deconinck. Cou[rtesy] Editions Condé Nast and the photog[ra-] pher, Paris. OPPOSITE BOTTOM, INS[ET:] President Reagan in sweat pants. 19[.] Photographer: Michael Evans. Cour[tesy] the photographer and The White Hou[se.]

Jock footwear knows many varia- tions, but the most common expression is the sneaker, once a simple canvas shoe with a pliable rubber sole. Although worn by the serious jock since its invention in 1892, it has since 1950 been adopt- ed by men of dubious athletic tendencies, such as Elvis Presley and Andy Warhol. The first sneak- ers, called Keds, were produced by the U.S. Rubber Company before the turn of the century. High- topped and made of brown canvas, the sneaker remained in the do- main of sports for the next fifty years. By mid-century, however, it had become a general recreational shoe. The jogging phenomenon emerged in the 1970s, and a dec- ade later, according to Esquire, there were 30 million joggers in the country, most of them wearing an up-to-date variation on the sneak- er, made of leather.

ABOVE: Andy Warhol in limo with sneak- ers. c. 1980. Photographer: Elliott Er- witt. Courtesy Magnum Photos, Inc. RIGHT: Elvis Presley in sneakers. c. 1956. Unknown photographer. Courtesy Kobal Collection.

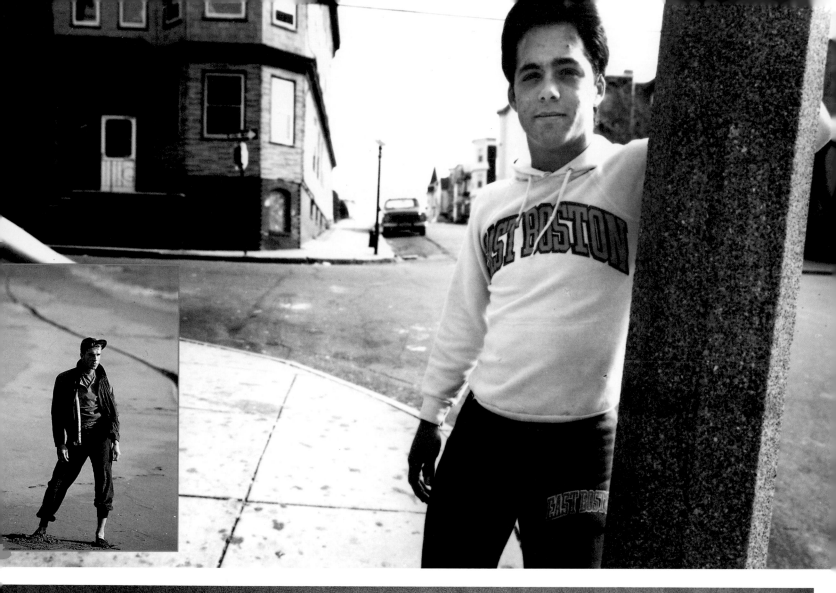

In an apparent indifference to style, the intellectual may choose sports clothing for its simplicity and comfort. Albert Einstein's informality bespeaks the relativity of modern clothing. Composer Quincy Jones, as cool as jazz and as confident as a credit-card endorsement, is likewise at ease in sweat clothes.

TOP LEFT: Albert Einstein. 1947. Photographer: Philippe Halsman. © 1989 Yvonne Halsman. BOTTOM LEFT: Quincy Jones for American Express. 1987. Advertisement. Courtesy American Express Company.

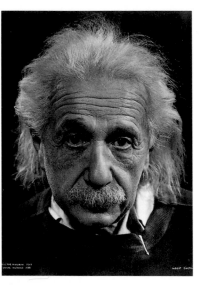

The designer Giorgio Armani has brought ordinary American sportswear into the realm of high fashion with relatively few design changes, all the while assimilating the informality that sports offer.

TOP RIGHT, BOTTOM RIGHT, and OPPOSITE: Sportswear by Emporio Armani. Fashion editorial published in Mondo Uomo, *Milan, September 1986. Photographer: Aldo Fallai. Courtesy Edizioni Edimoda S.p.A.*

THE NERD

Throughout the 1950s, Charles Atlas gave the skinny kid hope that he might transform himself from nerd to hero of the beach through a regimen of exercise. Atlas invented the term "ninety-seven pound weakling" to characterize the man seeking a future of facility and a good physique.

ABOVE: Advertisement for Charles Atlas, Ltd. c. 1955.

The nerd has risen from opprobrium to style supremacy. A fabricatic of the 1950s, he has been transmogrified from vilified style outcast paragon of advanced clothing. No hero in the postwar years, he rose stardom in a suite of films appropriately called *Revenge of the Nerds*, 1984 and 1987, and was the hero of an eponymous Broadway play, 1987. American society, once facile in its abnegation of the nerd, ha embraced him with zeal and approval. The role of the nerd has shifte from that of slide-rule-toting proto-scientist to savvy computer sp cialist, possessed of a knowledge all might envy. What he knows, r longer thought arcane, is now the way of the world. And with the con puter's technological triumph, the nerd has been insinuated into th world. His once notorious indifference to daily life, giving others prop cause for criticism and ostracism, has come to an end; with his assim lation into contemporary society, the shunning of the nerd (and h shunning of the world) is no longer viable. And the fashion compleme to these sociological changes is this: the characteristics of his style th once were most depreciated have been reevaluated, demonstrating th way in which perception creates and alters fashions in clothing ar appearance.

The etymology of "nerd" is not certain, but some have associated with "nerts," a polite form of "nuts," an expletive dating from the 192 or '30s, according to Eric Partridge. Mortimer Snerd, the dim-witte character created in 1939 by the ventriloquist and radio entertain Edgar Bergen, is also a possible source. Nerd describes someone foc ish, ineffectual, unsophisticated, socially inept, physically awkwar and even, as one dictionary added in 1973, an "unpleasant date." Ne describes a style that was unmitigatingly disparaged from the 1950s the 1970s. In the earlier decade, Alfred E. Neuman, freckled palad of *Mad Magazine*, represented for the junior-high audience the amiab risible characteristics of the nerd. Although unkempt and unattractiv he was to some a hero. In a decade when common goals were conformi and success, he was the eighth-grade version of the outcast as hero. H defiant "What, me worry?" cognition, so lacking in human intuition ar interaction, was to his audience courageous. Because male style rol tend to originate in adolescence, the nerd image, too, is initially fc mulated at puberty. It is a period when the adolescent undergoes a ki of rite of passage and chooses his role under the strident circumstanc of impolite, unsublimated, painfully cruel youth.

The nerd has had many incarnations, but some general characterist can be identified. The nerd is physically clumsy and lacks the grace the star athlete—thus the simple dialectic of jock and nerd. The ne is physically undeveloped, a variant of what Charles Atlas referred as "the ninety-seven pound weakling" who gets sand kicked in his fa on the beach. Further, the nerd is physically impaired. His awkwa frame, his lanky hair, and his too-big or too-little teeth, eyes, nose, ar mouth only exaggerate the irregularities of his style. If the model i fashion editorial for the Italian magazine *Per Lui* (March 1986) we judged by conventional standards, his prominent teeth, narrow eye bushy eyebrows, and glasses would make him a most unlikely candida for high fashion.

Such physical characteristics are exacerbated by another important trait of the nerd; he does not know how to present himself (nor how to secure his own physical comfort). When looking for warmth, he wears a sleeveless sweater, paradoxically leaving him with overheated chest and chilly extremities. He wears a short-sleeved shirt in a clinging, synthetic material, which only adds to his physical discomfort. A further note in this ill-fated wardrobe is the shirt buttoned to the collar but worn without a tie. In the 1950s, closing the top button of the shirt—a closure without function—was a coded signifier of the nerd; it was a denial of casualness in the decade of the casual. The distinctive nerdiness of the button phenomenon could only have occurred at a moment when collar buttons were customarily left open. Today the gesture has the power of a style statement because it is in opposition to the popular mode. Paradoxically, one has to be uncool to be really cool.

The nerd, oblivious to comfort and to a certain extent reliant upon the word of his ("yeeks!") mother to dress him, is a study in contradictions. The nerd would wear pants that are too short, suggesting a lack of self-assessment or a failure to look in the mirror. And the quintessential device of the nerd is the plastic pocket protector, or "nerdpak," a proletarian contraption that allows a pocket to be stuffed with pens, pencils, rulers, and slide rules or calculators. The assertively professional packing of this equipment would differentiate the nerd from the "big man on campus," the cool, self-sufficient, Levi's-wearing *bricoleur*, who has a single pen or pencil in his pocket sufficient to all needs. The nerd is the obsessive technocrat, filling his pockets with the job-specific equipment of contemporary proficiency.

In 1985, *Life Magazine* listed twenty-two identifying characteristics of the nerd: short haircut (receding hairline, large-domed forehead?); corrective lenses mended with adhesive tape (nearsighted?); rear-view mirror (on glasses); arrested case of acne with computer-terminal burn; goofy, toothy smile; generic T-shirt; pajama-print short-sleeved shirt (permanent press, bought by Mom?); plastic pocket guard (containing pens, plastic comb, eyeglass-cleaning papers, and air-pressure gauge); digital watch; belt cinched at the thorax; emergency pen carrier (suspended from waistband); Canon printout calculator (the neo-slide rule); embarrassing fly; computer traveling case; Hostess Cup Cakes; bag lunch (tuna fish on white, corn chips, Sno Balls); three-speed bike with bell, basket, and book clip; printout; unaffectedly short trousers (from high school); pants-leg clips; socks with heels worked down under the arches; and brown shoes. The image as viewed by *Life* is hardly beguiling, but the genuine article is even more elaborate. Other characteristics might include a clashing, notably unsuccessful pattern mix; a cap with visor that shifts to the sides or rear; and the omnipresent glasses, not only broken and mended with adhesive tape but also ill-fitting and tending to slide down the face, emphasizing irregular features, as well.

Glasses are appropriate for the nerd not only because they signal the failure of his body to function in the seemingly invulnerable jock mode but because they hold an almost iconic power; glasses are what the bully pulls off in his taunts; glasses are what slip off at the water fountain; and in their distortion of the eyes, glasses create a focus on the pain of the nerd. The nerd style evokes sympathy. One readily distinguished the nerd in the 1950s, a decade when winners seemed clearly differentiated from losers. The awkwardness, lack of internal and external ease, and signs of social marginality served to make the nerd an ideal pariah. The added insult of spiky hair, indifference to proper bathing and hygiene, and the ubiquitous trail of paper from the shoe seemed to qualify the nerd for a lifetime of opprobrium.

In the 1980s, however, the nerd has returned trailing not scraps of paper but glory. In an issue of the magazine *Elle* (March 1988), fashion writer Kathleen Beckett-Young recognized "nerd chic," comment-

Rock-and-roll singer Buddy Holly dressed in a conservative style for his performances in the 1950s, but his self-assured look provided a model for the spectacles-wearing adolescent.

RIGHT: Buddy Holly. c. 1958. Photographer: James J. Kriegsmann. Courtesy Magnum Photos, Inc.

alian fashion took the nerd to the ach in 1986. Fumbling and in- t, inappropriately dressed (even designer clothes), he makes a o-handed catch in a game of fris- e, one of the few nerd sports in use of a plastic disk and absence team play. The young man in a ttoned-up shirt with no tie, also m Italian fashion, sports the othy smile and dark-rimmed sses of the nerd. In mid-decade, American magazine found the rd phenomenon so compelling, ove, that it set out to identify his aracteristics, beginning with his ack-framed glasses, short pants, d plastic pocket liner.

ing: "Dork, spaz, geek, creep, nerd. When we were kids, we sneered at them. Or worse, feared we were one of them. But today their high-water pants, white socks, clunky black shoes, and thick glasses are everywhere. Irony of ironies, the look of the moment is the look most of us tried hard to avoid while were growing up. Take heart, nerds, your fifteen minutes are here."

To be sure, the nerd has always been capable of transformation. In the comic strips, Clark Kent, wearing dark-rimmed glasses, could step into a telephone booth and emerge as Superman; by sending away for the Charles Atlas kit, the scrawny child could guarantee that hereafter no one would again kick sand in his face. Perhaps bravado masculinity has always been the alter ego of the nerd, even though sensitivity and vulnerability would have been more immediately apparent.

There have been nerds in the arts as well as in technology and the sciences. The conservative image of rock-and-roll singer Buddy Holly, whose brief career ended in 1959 when he died in a plane crash, was in extreme opposition to the glittering, ostentatious styles of many performers of the day. As Stephen Fried, a writer for *GQ*, recalled: "Jet black frames were for geeks and Buddy Holly fans," an identification of style with the plaintiveness of the music, perhaps; that association was not lost on subsequent musicians, such as Elvis Costello and Buster Poindexter, in the 1980s. But the preeminent nerd exemplar is the filmmaker and actor Woody Allen, whose disheveled elegance and protean creative talent identify the nerd aspiration. Even as Allen has appropriated many traditional garments, such as Oxford-cloth shirts with button-down collars, his use of the fashion materials has placed them in the sympathetic context of the nerd style.

PASSION FOR WORK

Woody Allen's style followers are legion. Although some might believe that he reached supremacy only in *Annie Hall* (1977), where the Ralph Lauren clothing he selected for his star, Diane Keaton, instantly created a style, his personal impact is more substantive and sustained than that of his heroine. Among his progeny are the style-aware students of the vanguard Paris fashion school, Studio Berçot. Assembling outfits from their own designs as well as from ready-to-wear clothing, they emulate the nerd through such assimilated appearances as high-water pants, heavy shoes, oversized garments, and large, black glasses. At an antic extreme is a solicitation for the trendy journal *PAPER* (1984), which is clothed in the stereotype of a toothy, unkempt nerd. The person least likely to have been invited to the teen party of the 1950s is the celebrant and the celebrated figure several generations later. Likewise, a liqueur, La Grande Passion, in an advertising appeal to the style conscious, portrays the Clark Kent-style nerd in a St. Vitus dance of business success, passion for work, and a combination of the fun and the serious.

If the nerd's lack of agility had ostracized him from the games of the 1950s, he played with a new definition of dexterity in the 1980s. In June 1986 a fashion feature for *Per Lui*—which is directed, one presumes, at young men who would not yet have been born in the 1950s—brings the overdressed nerd to the edge of the water, his feet neither bare nor casually shod but wearing street shoes so ungainly as to force him to catch the frisbee with two hands rather than one. Muscle beach has manifestly been replaced by geek beach. It is the triumph of the nerd in the most unlikely of places—in the fashion magazine and at the seaside, where physical prowess had hitherto prevailed and the nerd, in prior generations, had been terrorized. The improbability of this triumph is made more apparent by examining the lineage of our hero.

The sad, struggling figure played by Jerry Lewis in a film called *The Patsy* (1964) wore the awkwardness and dress of the nerd. Lewis followed a long tradition in comedy of presenting a type in ill-fitting clothing and spectacles, his bearing ungainly, his behavior without finesse. Some twenty years later, however, the nerd has been more sympathetically incarnated as Pee-wee Herman, the children's comedian and cult hero, an underdog of physical limpness wearing too-tight suits. His passive-aggressive manner lends the nerd role a goofy, harmless demeanor, also realized in the character of Hornby K. Fletcher, a "Rent-a-Nerd" created in New York by actor Mike McDonald in 1987. Like others in the national organization of nerds, whose membership is open to all craving the collective identity of nerd, Hornby K. Fletcher is lovable, a figure to be welcomed, not shunned. Recognizing the transformation of the image, advertising as well as fashion has thus turned to the glorification of the nerd.

The nerd has also become a sexual creature, vulnerable and feeling, a perfect partner because he is not only concerned with himself. In the film *Revenge of the Nerds* (1984), a young woman commends one of the characters on his sexual performance, and he reminds her that nerds don't spend their spare time in self-centered exercising to keep themselves muscular; they think about sex. A male counterpart to Cinderella, the nerd blossoms in a seductive relationship with a woman.

In the 1980s, creatures in the nerd image may still wear their glasses and clunky shoes, but they also wear the most advanced fashions of the

The nerd was lionized in the 1980s. Pressed into service in promoting a liqueur and a magazine, he would also figure as the central character in a play. Filmmaker Woody Allen, whose wit and style gave the awkward young intellectual in dark-rimmed glasses hope for romance and even fame, was the nerd exemplar. Even young students from the Paris fashion school Studio Berçot would wear glasses, boots, and shirts in the nerd style.

OPPOSITE TOP: Advertisement for La Grande Passion Liqueur. 1987. Photographer: Richard Pandiscio. Courtesy PAPER Publishing Company. OPPOSITE CENTER: Woody Allen. 1969. Photographer: Philippe Halsman. © 1989 Yvonne Halsman. OPPOSITE BOTTOM: Fashion students from the Studio Berçot, Paris. Published in Accent, Paris, Winter 1987. Photographer: Scott Osman. Courtesy the photographer. ABOVE LEFT: Advertisement for PAPER Magazine. 1984. Photographer: Jon Ericson. Courtesy PAPER Publishing Company.

ABOVE RIGHT: Robert Joy stars in the 1987 play The Nerd. *Photographer: Gerry Goodstein. Courtesy the photographer.*

times. The nerd look was brought to high style in mid-decade, and what would have seemed unacceptable ten years before was now found to be in the vanguard. The apotheosis of the nerd may be the natural consequence of the waning physical culture of recent years. Perhaps the stock-market decline of October 1987 has underlined the failure of bravado masculinity in business and renewed the need for brains and acumen. When primacy is given to intelligence over the body, the nerd is logically drawn from the forlorn, marginal limits, to which he was restricted in the 1950s, to the very center of the stylistic imagination, as in the 1980s.

Is the nerd as indifferent to style as the 1950s might have imagined? Or, alternatively, is the nerd style an astutely ironic look at fashion? The extremes of style definition that the nerd has achieved suggests a greater self-consciousness than was heretofore ascribed to him. Perhaps nerd styles are like the brief efflorescence of Oxford bags in 1925–26, when wide white pants were a fad in men's clothing of England and the

e-wee Herman, who devised a
evision personality in the 1980s
t combined boyish exuberance
h fastidiousness and propriety,
sses in a suit that is too small,
phasizing his man-child quality.

OSITE: Pee-wee Herman. Published in
uel, Paris, June 1987. Photographer:
ier Lambours. Courtesy the photog-
her.

A French fashion magazine for men has added to the nerd's lineage, at left above presenting him in dandified cummerbund and ascot and at right casting him for a part in *Tom Brown's School Days,* where he would be marked for ostracism in his high-water pants, circular dark-rimmed glasses, slicked-down hair, and thick-soled shoes.

ABOVE LEFT: Jacket by Façonnable; shirt
with cummerbund by Jean-François
Charles for Piero Panchetti. Fashion ed-
itorial published in Vogue Hommes
International, *Paris, Fall–Winter*
1987–88. Photographer: Kim Knott.
Courtesy Publications Condé Nast S.A.
ABOVE RIGHT: Suit by Jean-Paul Gaul-
tier; tie, socks, and brogues by Comme des

Garçons. Fashion editorial published in
Vogue Hommes International, *Paris,*
Fall–Winter 1987–88. Photographer:
Kim Knott. Courtesy Publications Condé
Nast S.A.

United States. Exaggerations and irony prevailed in clothing that was purposely ridiculous. Indeed, nearly sixty years later, in 1984, the musician David Byrne, himself a nerd hero, created the big suit in an instinctive reflection of Oxford bags and a cognitive appreciation of oversizing in men's clothing. Byrne, the intelligent hero, is no less a nerd style figure than Buddy Holly had been, but his sanctioning of the style is an extreme gesture of individuality, as well.

There is a Walter Mitty dream in everyone. There is also a Superman beneath the unassuming guise of the nerd, who is both the sympathetic everyman and the supreme expression of style as its own victory.

The cult of the nerd reached such proportions in 1987 that a second film called *Revenge of the Nerds* was released, and a party service called "Rent-a-Nerd" came into being. Michael Boodro, an observer of the social scene, wrote in *Express* in the spring of 1983: "The new style instills power and strength into the weakest and most despised stereotypes, the wimp, loser, and nerd, by resuscitating their paraphernalia." Almost Old Testament in his moralizing vengeance, he found this new disposition of nerd to be without style change but with revised style values.

ABOVE: Robert Carradine stars in Revenge of the Nerds II: Nerds in Paradise. *1987. Photographer: Zade Rosenthal. Courtesy Twentieth Century Fox.*
ABOVE RIGHT: Mike McDonald as "Rent-a-Nerd." Published in People, *New York, May 25, 1987. Photographer: Kevin Horan. Courtesy Time Inc.*

In his movies of the 1950s and
'60s, actor Jerry Lewis perfected
the role of the nerd. Whether his
characters were bunglers or vic-
tims, their vulnerability was em-
pathic.

RIGHT: Jerry Lewis in The Patsy. *1964.
Unknown photographer for Paramount
Pictures. Courtesy Kobal Collection.*

As Buddy Holly was a style leader
in the 1950s, so rock singer David
Byrne would take up the cudgel in
the 1980s. Donning oversize clothing not unlike the Oxford bags
worn by collegians some sixty years
before, he affects the child-man
quality of the nerd, playing out the
child's fantasy of assuming dad's
clothing.

ABOVE LEFT AND RIGHT: David Byrne in
Stop Making Sense. *1984. Photographer: Adelle Lutz. Courtesy the photographer. RIGHT: Lawrence E. Dews
wearing Oxford bags made by a Los Angeles tailor. December 21, 1925. Unknown photographer. Courtesy Bettmann
Archive.*

Languorous and awkward, unde-
fined in posture, he who might
have been a wallflower became no-
ticed in the fashion magazines of
the 1980s. The nerd, once the outcast and the rejected, was granted
social acceptance and style leadership. Black socks and dress shoes
with shorts and slicked-back wet
hair were given authority precisely
because they once represented
lack of authority.

*RIGHT: Cardigan by Paul Smith; shirt by
Replay; Bermudas by Cutty Sark; tie by
Dionisio. Fashion editorial published in
Per Lui, Milan, April 1987. Photogra-
pher: Mario Testino. Courtesy Edizione
Conde Nast S.p.A. BELOW: Shirt by Top
Man; sweater by Dries van Noter; trousers
by English Eccentrics. Fashion editorial
published in Arena, London, Winter
1987–88. Photographer: Kim Knott.
Courtesy Wagadon Ltd.*

THE WORKER

In the history of fashion, two opposing schemes have been devised to describe the development of a style; in one it is said that a style idea may originate at the "top" (in terms of economic and social classes), therefrom to "trickle down"; at the other extreme, it is said that it may swell from below, from vernacular dress or street fashion (as well as from the clothing of the "lower" classes), to influence, at a later date or by distant remove, the "upper" levels of dress. Although this opposition has been formulated chiefly with respect to women's clothing, it may apply in a like sense, but with little certainty and conflicting evidence, to men's clothing, as well.

The functional dress of the worker has held an ever-widening appeal for men in the twentieth century, even as the traditional categories of labor have narrowed. Nevertheless, the worker has originated much of the clothing adopted by men in other fields. An indeterminate *nostalgie de la boue*, a desire to be more simple and of the proletariat, is a compelling factor for men today, preeminently in selecting clothing for leisure activity; men have learned from the functionalism of the laborer's style of dress and have advanced the imagery of the worker beyond toil to grace. This transformation of working attire to a more bourgeois leisure, this collaging of elements, has played a vital role in the twentieth century. Jeans, which are derived from the world of labor, have been paired with manifestly high-style, expensive shirts; the cotton T-shirt, no longer merely the underwear of the laborer, has become a luxury, its fabrication at times fancy rather than only functional.

Even in the transformation of the garment, its political content remains intact. Thus, during the early 1970s, when members of protest movements adopted the clothing of workers, this would seem to have represented an identification with the worker, establishing the affiliation of the protester with the people. In a 1972 photograph of protestors in New York opposing United States involvement in Southeast Asia, the demonstrators are garbed in jeans and military-surplus clothing, the ascendant styles at the time by which disestablishment sentiment was expressed. Despite being freshly perceived as protest clothing in the early 1970s, however, jeans began a rapid style migration to urban and

...farmer and his child standing ...nd in hand suggest the heroism ...John Steinbeck's Joad family ...d the gritty tragedy of American ...e in the 1930s. Photographed for ...advertising campaign for de-...ner jeans, the image shimmers ...th the immutable realism of the ...nerican heartland and suggests ...well the abiding dignity of the ...nerican worker.

...OVE: Advertisement for Guess? jeans by ...orges Marciano. 1986. Photographer: ...n Griffiths. Courtesy Guess? by Georges ...rciano.

Establishment behaviors by the end of the decade. Meanwhile, the had been an expression of democracy in clothing that escaped fashio by being a classic and by being inexpensive and universal.

From the beginning of the century, the overall (and, alternatively the coverall) served as the sign of the worker, its practical materials an adaptable style fulfilling a need for working wear. The overall was tr ditionally a type of loose trousers worn over others as a protection fro soil, wear, or weather. Made of a durable fabric in standard colors, ofte blue denim or the striped cotton of mattress ticking, the overall is cha acteristically a garment with bib and suspenders. It had been adapte in the nineteenth century to use for children, who more typically wo the garment with sleeves and collar known as the coverall. Women clothing also included variations on the overall, particularly with tl sudden enlistment of women in factory work during the Second Wor War, and the imagery of "Rosie the Riveter" outfitted in overal quickly developed. Men found that the bib front of the overall accor modated a number of pockets, and the loose fit provided for easy sizir in ordering by mail, as well as in wear over trousers.

In a J. C. Leyendecker cover for the Labor Day issue of *The America Weekly*, in 1946, the worker is triumphant over the newly peaceful worl his overalls complemented by a chambray work shirt and heavy, lace boots. This particular worker represents organized labor. His attir manifestly taken from the functional clothing of workers, whether u ban or rural, members of a union or independent, is expressly intende as a sign of the laborer. The Leyendecker man further wears a visore cap and holds a sledge hammer in suggestion of outdoor, manual wor even as he surmounts the world of organized labor. The imagery of tl farmer (and to some extent the laborer) had been galvanized in Ameri between 1937 and 1943 by the Farm Security Administration (FS photographers in their documentation of American rural life. In th program sponsored by the Works Progress Administration of the Fe eral government, the common clothing of work was made evident straightforward photography of farmers and laborers in communiti across the country.

The romantic transformations of the overall are extensive. Its ru service and its universalizing of the dignity of labor were suggested its revitalization in the 1960s and 1970s, when it was worn in civil-rigl marches and antiwar protests. In wearing the light duck-cloth versio of house-painter's pants, artists have adopted the garb of the laborer a thus reaffirmed the dignity of work. The manual laborer is likewi celebrated by Herb Ritts in a series of photographs called Men at Wc (1987). In this case a standing figure, his body bare from the waist u achieves a mythic presence through his physical energy and his po: as well as through his clothing—his leather apron, coveralls, and hea boots—which establish a continuity with the world of work.

The full regalia of country clothing was worn by President Jimr Carter in the late 1970s, evoking the working-class sensibility of t earlier years of the decade and referring to his own role as the sole farn president of the century (as well as to the agrarian idealism of Jeff sonian democracy). President Carter's preference for jeans and cha bray work shirts was a sign of his identification with the worker. In i agery, the outfit recalled the clothing worn by farm workers in Russ Lee's FSA photographs of the South and Middle West, but an ad tional political twist was that it quietly invoked New Deal magnanimi The shirt of blue chambray, its seams reinforced by double stitchi and its fabric growing more and more supple and agreeable the mor is worn, provided a paradigm of work clothing in use and in image Although the self-conscious reconstruction of a small-town herit: reached its apogee in the clothing imagery of President Carter—c. turing the spirit, for example, of photographer Michael Disfarmc formal portraits of the men of his Arkansas community—individ members of various professions have continued to sustain the rural a laboring references of overalls and work shirts, most especially Jan Taylor and Willie Nelson in the performing arts, Haystack Calhou sports, and Carl Andre in the visual arts.

The postwar period established a new language of jeans, the m

During the social rebellions that bridged the decades of the 1960s and 1970s, college students and other young protestors appropriated the clothing of the worker, recognizing in its unequivocal social connotations a symbol for their struggle.

ABOVE: New York demonstration against the blockade of North Vietnam. 1972. Photographer: Charles Harbutt. Courtesy Archive Pictures Inc.

fluential clothing in contemporary dress. The new language addressed
nineteenth-century category of clothing but it attributed to jeans
twentieth-century social values. Appropriated from the work pants invented by Levi Strauss during the Gold Rush era of the 1850s, jeans
were known only as work clothing until the Second World War.

The early history of jeans is an American myth of epic retelling and
retailing. According to legend, a wise prospector for gold told the dry-
goods merchant Levi Strauss, arriving in California during the early
1850s, that rather than transporting this cargo of brown canvas for tents
and wagon covers, he would have done better to bring pants. Strauss
used the canvas to make trousers suitable to the rough work of digging
for gold, and his Levi's became the eponymous jeans of decades to follow. Within a short time Strauss adopted a staunch French cotton twill
loomed in Nîmes (thus denim, *de Nîmes*), giving his trousers flexibility
and fit.

Identified with the American West, jeans were brought back to the
East Coast as Western-wear souvenirs in the 1930s, when dude ranches
in the West were enjoying considerable popularity. During the same
era (and even before), Hollywood's characteristic conflation of the casual and the Western provided heroes in jeans. Throughout this period,
the fundamental attributes of the sturdy denim trousers remained sta-
ble. Strauss had changed the color from brown to blue in 1873, when
he also registered his trademark; but the classic 501 Levi's blue jeans
were marked with the same lot number Levi Strauss had assigned them
in the nineteenth century.

In the years following the Second World War, jeans would be subject
to a wide range of modifications and variations. In the late 1960s, flared
bottoms appropriated from the bell-bottom ampleness of sailor pants
yielded to elephant bells, with connotations of protest. Likewise, embroidered and decorated jeans of the late 1960s and early 1970s beto-
kened rebellion and provided a facile differentiation from those worn
by workers. If the jeans of the popular Woodstock Music Festival, in
1969, outfitted communal love and freedom, the enterprises of love
were in little time fitted more erotically and commercially by artist Andy
Warhol into his design for the cover of *Sticky Fingers* (1971), an album
released by the Rolling Stones. Placing jeans squarely within the domain of the male, the album cover had a functioning fly crafted around
the form of Joe Dallesandro, thus more than fulfilling the concept of
jeans as the life mold of the wearer. Warhol's emphasis on eroticism
rather than functionalism became the fundamental identification of the
garment for the decade, an era of jeans eroticism for both sexes.

In the language of the second half of the twentieth century, it might
be suggested that jeans have binary social identities, on the one hand
fulfilling a function that is collective and symbolic and on the other hand
playing a role that is personal and physical. In discussing the latter
identity, the fashion authority John Berendt rightly referred to jeans as
"body sculpture," realizing that as they are worn, each pair takes on the
form of the person who wears them. In the early 1970s, when jeans were
at their peak in popularity, this potential was realized by both men and
women in the wearing of exceptionally tight jeans, sometimes accom-
plished by shrinking them on the body in a hot bath. Even without the
wish of shrinking, the impress of the body within plays a role in the
form of the jeans and thus offers an indication of the individual within.
As for their symbolic identity, the United States, the American West,
independence, informality, and sensuality are frequently cited as attributes of the garment. As items of men's apparel, jeans convey messages that may seem to be mixed and disharmonious. In the 1950s, for
instance, jeans were associated with both the American West and disestablishment behavior. Their wholesome probity came under challenge when they became associated with youth and rebellion, as in the
55 play (and subsequent movie) *Blue Denim*. But the link between
denim and youthful rebellion was almost tenuous; more dramatic was
the sundering of the indigenous Americana of jeans. In the 1970s, the
style leader and observer of the social scene Diana Vreeland reportedly
named jeans as the most important fashion of the century. If so, they
represented American ascendancy in the century.

The rawness of rural life in the
1930s found expression in the
images of workers taken by Farm
Security Administration photographers. As in the dour paintings of
Grant Wood and other American
Regionalists, the utilitarian garments of the worker symbolized
the virtues of the American farm
and its productivity, making a
claim for agrarian dignity and social
justice.

*ABOVE: Farm Security Administration
client and his sons, Caruthersville, Mis-
souri. 1938. Photographer: Russell Lee.
Courtesy Library of Congress.*

Specific features of a pair of overalls—the stout cotton drill, deep
pockets, metal buttons, fortifying
rivets, and double-stitched, reinforced seams—substantiate the
possibility of work in clothing such
as this and grant a proletarian aura
to the wearer.

*ABOVE: Freedom March on Washington,
D.C., August 28, 1963. Published in
Life, New York, September 6, 1963.
Photographer: Paul Schutzer. Courtesy
Time Inc.*

By the 1970s, jeans had gone international, and denim made in th[e] United States came close to being world currency. Consumers arou[nd] the globe specifically sought American labor and styling. In 1973, Le[vi] Strauss & Co. would ration its denim jeans in world markets, owing [to] the lack of cotton and of manufacturing capability to meet the seeming[ly] insatiable demand. From time to time in the postwar period, the prim[e] black-market commodity of exchange with Iron Curtain and Thi[rd] World countries had been American jeans, their prestige worth mo[re] than dollars and their currency being the American experience.

This sweeping, universal acceptance of jeans in the 1970s led to the[ir] approbation throughout the male wardrobe. Warhol himself served [as] avatar of the denim style in his hybrid connections with art, society, a[nd] popular culture. In 1980, briefly under contract to a New York mod[el] agency, Warhol appeared in jeans on the cover of the Italian fashi[on] magazine *L'Uomo Vogue* (June–July), symbolizing the style he ha[d] helped to validate a decade before.

Michael Disfarmer's photographic chronicle of the men in the small Southern town of Heber Springs, Arkansas, during the Second World War is an essay in style. On this occasion, although the men are not at work, they are dressed for it. The figure at left wears true work clothing, but the others are literally "white collar" workers. Their clothes equalize the effect, however, in the informality of their rolled cuffs, open collars, and unpressed style.

ABOVE: Three working men. c. 1940.
Photographer: Michael Disfarmer.
Courtesy Staley-Wise Gallery.

Herb Ritts's photograph of a garage mechanic in coveralls is like[-] wise an essay in style.

OPPOSITE: Body Shop: Fred. 19[.]
Photographer: Herb Ritts. Cour[tesy]
Staley-Wise Gallery.

The 1980s witnessed the return of jeans to their associations with working and the working class. A chain of stores called The Gap advertised its own brand of denim trousers (known as "Workforce" clothing) in photographs calling to mind the farm workers of the 1930s as depicted by the great FSA photographers; indeed, one of the most celebrated photographers, Dorothea Lange, was represented in the ads. The dignity of labor, it was implied, inheres in jeans, and if that dignity has been tarnished by rebellious attitudes and behaviors, it nonetheless can be restored and burnished by recalling the noble history of the garment.

Rock-singer Bruce Springsteen asserted an intense, working-class iconography through jeans that dodged the 1970s in a return to style origins. His blue-jeans persona—the cover of his album *Born in the U.S.A.* (1984) depicts him in Levi's, white T-shirt, and Western belt— is like that of the jeans market of the 1980s, which returned to classic forms, the principle makers, and traditional associations with the garment, as if to deny that the style variations and eroticized jeans had ever happened. This tendency in men's clothing for styles to return to their origins, divesting themselves, as it were, of recent associations, is rare in other design disciplines. Thus the history of jeans has displayed a special style set that have may receded but never wholly disappeared. A flood of decoration, erotica, staining, specialty washing, distressing, and fitting may come and go, but jeans remain a vital symbol of the working man.

Nevertheless, an aberrant phenomenon of the 1970s was the emergence of so-called designer jeans. Chiefly found in women's wear, they originated in the French preference for close-fitting pants, which became available in America through the French Jean Shop. In 1977, an American company began to mass-produce French-style jeans under the name of Jordache (selected by the owners, the Nakash brothers, to imply French elegance; no specific designer was connected with the company), and soon the designer designation caught on. By 1979, more than thirty designers—notably Gloria Vanderbilt and Calvin Klein— as well as a famous discothèque, Studio 54, were associated with jeans for men and women. In 1982 alone, the peak year of the phenomenon, some 22 million pairs of designer jeans were sold. Most were at least twice as expensive as the conventional product (which had been popular, in large part, because of its low price), and some versions soared to four times the cost of regular jeans. More a fad than a sustained fashion, designer jeans (*The New York Times* preferred to call them "status jeans") reached a wide audience through advertising on radio and television. Often erotic in tone (the young model Brooke Shields intoned in a television commercial: "Nothing comes between me and my Calvins"), the advertisements offered provocativeness as a goal. Ironically, the sustained alliance of jeans with high fashion would also help return them to their sources in the 1980s. Throughout the decade, Calvin Klein's jeans advertising diminished its eroticism and reestablished a Western correlation. In like manner, Ralph Lauren, who reverted to the redolently exotic, historicist word "dungarees," even cast a contemporary design mogul in the role of cowboy. And a company that enigmatically styled itself "Guess?" left no question of its nostalgia for the 1930s, the West, and the small town in advertising that convened a pickup truck, a Ford, and jeans with Western boots and ten-gallon hats. As the designer-jeans fad subsided, denim trousers reverted to the style at their matrix.

Ancillary to the image of the worker and cowboy in jeans is the romantic vision of the artist in paint-spattered overalls. A source for that imagery may be a 1949 photograph of Abstract Expressionist painter Jackson Pollock, who was born in Cody, Wyoming, and had the striding physicality of the American West. In time the protective garment became its own icon, and by the 1980s painter variations had migrated through art movements to such artists as Mike Bidlo, who had appropriated Pollock's art in his early work, and James Mathers, who, rolling his cuffs not with J. Alfred Prufrock temerity but with James Dean audacity, allowed his painterly labor to be evident from his jeans. The romantic stirrings that had a century before banished artists to garrets

coveralls represent the urban laborer, the work shirt symbolizes [the] farm laborer. President Jimmy [Car]ter wears the chambray shirt [pre]ferred by farmers in the American South. Chambray (named after [the] town of Cambrai, in France, [wh]ere it was first used for sunbon[ne]ts) is a plain-weave cotton with [col]ored warp and white filling. In [wo]rk clothing, the colored warp is [ordi]narily blue, and the effect is to [cre]ate a garment in the manner of a [dre]ss shirt, yet one manifestly in[cor]rect for a boardroom. The slight [va]riations in the fabric also suggest [th]e uniqueness of hand-loomed [clo]th, even though chambray is [ma]ss-produced.

THE **American** WEEKLY

Greatest Circulation in the World

"The Nation's Reading Habit" Magazine Section—New York Journal-American Copyright, 1946, by American Weekly, Inc. All Rights Reserved.

Week of Sept. 1, 1946

LABOR DAY

[Illu]strator J. C. Leyendecker [ex]poitly exploited the heroic im[age]s of the 1930s farm worker in [a] 1946 portrayal of the modern [lab]orer in overalls. Contrary to the [jo]b in this popular rendition, [ho]wever, factories had long en[cou]raged the use of the one-piece [ov]erall in avoidance of garments [wit]h straps that could be caught in [the] machinery. At the turn of the [cen]tury, coveralls were identified [as] "boiler suits" and "mechanics' [ove]ralls."

brought the American artist in the second half of the century to working-class nobility in denim.

Working life has added another romantic image to the style vocabulary of the male. The T-shirt, a sleeved, collarless undershirt worn by the worker, was initially a protective inner layer of clothing that was a counterpart to the overall as the outer layer. Although the T-shirt might be revealed at work, under other circumstances it was to remain concealed. In the early part of the century, the Sears, Roebuck & Co. mail-order catalogue advertised the T-shirt for its utility as an undergarment, but in the 1930s, began to suggest the possibility of the shirt's exposure. Still appearing within the pages of underwear advertising, it was listed as the "gob"-style shirt of the sailor, who wore it while working aboard ship. The outer garment, or blouse, could be kept clean and pressed if the T-shirt was worn for heavy work. This romantic association with the sea, added to the ideal of cleanliness, allowed the T-shirt to emerge for limited use in its own right.

An even more romantic version of the T-shirt's exposure can be traced to a specific time and place. When Tennessee Williams's play *A Streetcar Named Desire* premiered in New York on December 3, 1947, the T-shirt achieved visibility and sensuality. Director Elia Kazan affirmed that the garment had been selected for Marlon Brando in the Stanley Kowalski role not by Williams's prior stage direction but because Brando wore a T-shirt to rehearsals. Its identity was that of the worker at leisure; wearing a collared shirt in public, he resorted to his T-shirt at home—in Kowalski's case, of course, not a picturesquely domestic setting. When the film version was released in 1951, the entire country would come to recognize Brando's T-shirt image. His T-shirt was the expression of the male, as patently revealing of his masculinity as the clinging cotton was in defining his musculature. Like jeans, the T-shirt can articulate the body in significant ways, defining the torso, and, as the sleeves ride up, revealing the biceps, which otherwise would be concealed even in a short-sleeved shirt with collar. Brando's T-shirt, so revealing of his animal presence, was an interpretation of the T-shaped skivvie brought home by military men after the Second World War, but it now assumed a sensuous role unknown in the company of men at war.

In *The Wild One* (1954), a controversial film about a marauding motorcycle gang in California, Brando would further enhance the image of the T-shirt. For this role jeans, leather jacket, and the T-shirt converged to form an icon of rebellion that has endured to the present day. Brando further expanded the T-shirt's possibilities by wearing it with an outer garment without benefit of an intermediate shirt with collar. By 1956, the year when *The Man in the Gray Flannel Suit* was released on film, the lines between white collar and the collarless T-shirt were clearly drawn. The contrast had been heightened by the appearance of James Dean the year before in *Rebel without a Cause*, wearing the T-shirt independently—or with a windbreaker on which the collar was slightly rolled. Dean symbolized the rebellion of youth, and the role was encoded in a succession of films about the kid hoodlum in T-shirt and jacket with raised collar. The threatening delinquent would leave the house in a shirt without a collar, thus expressing his defiance of propriety and of mom's surveillance and gentle handling.

More delicate than delinquent, the young Truman Capote wore the T-shirt without the affront of the screen miscreants, in part because its free-flowing lines did not define the body. The loose T-shirt was acceptable as boy's apparel, and even though Capote was past adolescence when photographed by Henri Cartier-Bresson in 1947, he presented a childlike lack of menace. The view of John F. Kennedy relaxing in the garden of his Washington home in the mid-1950s indicates that leisure use of the T-shirt was possible and that its clean whiteness could also be associated with wholesome values.

Two decades later, the T-shirt had become not so much a sign in its own right as a signpost for the messages it carried. It displayed graphics and slogans, and offered possibilities that were contingent on the T-shirt's visibility. To convey the graphic message, the shirt had to be visible externally. In some sense an extension of the jersey worn by the

Continued on page 62

From the middle of the nineteenth century, the merchant Levi Strauss made work pants for gold miners, lumberjacks, and other men engaged in outdoor labor. Although his 501 blue jeans have a rugged, proletarian history, they have been fully assimilated into recreational clothing and urban style.

CENTER: Lumberjacks wearing Levi Strauss jeans. c. 1900. Unknown photographer. Courtesy Levi Strauss Archive. TOP, BOTTOM, AND OPPOSITE: Three images from advertisement for Levi's 501 Blues. 1987. Photographer: Claude Jaques. Courtesy Levi Strauss & Co.

A chain of stores called The Gap stakes a claim in history through imagery. Employing Western photography, its advertising campaign for its line of Workforce clothing moves from a classic documentary image by Farm Security Administration photographer Dorothea Lange to similar images of its own brand of clothing today. The same campaign presented a list of those who wear jeans, naming white-collar workers and professionals as well as the traditional categories of worker. Whether a meteorologist, teacher, lawyer, real-estate broker, librarian, nurse, architect, astronaut, doctor, or chemist, all were to dress as "the American worker,"

at least on their weekends of leisure.

LEFT: Cafe near Pinole, Californi 1956. Photographer: Dorothea Lan Collection Oakland Museum. Depicted advertisement for The Gap's Workfo clothing. 1987. Courtesy The Gap I BELOW AND OPPOSITE: Three images fr advertisement for The Gap's Workfo clothing. 1987. Photographer: Lar Staedler. Courtesy The Gap Inc.

54

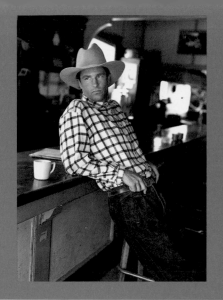

on of post-1960s American art
d culture, Andy Warhol brought
gh art and high style to jeans.
heritor of the tradition of the
nerican artist as pioneer (in the
nner of Jackson Pollock), War-
l had a streak of Bohemianism
at was overlaid with strong traces
Americana, preppy good-boy
le, and business acumen. A gen-
e American innocent in the arts,
found his imagery in popular
irces and his excitement in the
roism of celebrity. Warhol was
h Natty Bumpo and Nathaniel
st, a disheveled, common-man
smopolite of postwar American

*OSITE: Andy Warhol. c. 1980. Pho-
apher: Evelyn Hofer. Courtesy Ar-
e Pictures Inc. TOP RIGHT: Artist
son Pollock. Published in* Life, *New
k, August 8, 1949. Photographer:
tha Holmes. Courtesy Time Inc.
TER RIGHT: Painter James Mathers
Rose's Lime Juice. 1985. Advertise-
t. Photographer: Perry Ogden. Cour-
Rose's Lime Juice (Cadbury-
weppes, Inc.). BOTTOM RIGHT:
ter Mike Bidlo in front of his version
latisse's* La Danse. *1985. Photog-
her: Jeannette Barron. Courtesy
y-Wise Gallery.*

The Rolling Stones's most celebrated album cover was *Sticky Fingers* (1971), designed by Andy Warhol and Craig Braun using Warhol's Polaroid photographs of a man in jeans. Provocative in its time, the front cover unzips to reveal grisaille Jockey shorts. Indicative of the sexual incitement of the era, the design is echoed in Bruce Springsteen's album cover for *Born in the U.S.A.* (1984), but the erotic temperature is lowered; the singer is viewed from the back in white

T-shirt, worn Levi's, and Western belt, a red visored cap stuck in his hip pocket.

ABOVE, LEFT AND CENTER: Cover for the Rolling Stones album Sticky Fingers. *1971. Art director: Craig Braun. Photographer: Andy Warhol. Courtesy Atco Records.* ABOVE RIGHT: *Cover for the Bruce Springsteen album* Born in the U.S.A. *1984. Art director and designer: Andrea Klein. Photographer: Annie Leibovitz. Courtesy Columbia Records.*

Young teenagers photographed in 1958, above, and Andy Warhol posing for a fashion-magazine cover in 1980, opposite, wear jeans that are closer in style than the bell-bottom model sported by the young man above right, in attendance at the Woodstock Music Festival of 1969, when exaggerated forms were the jeans fashion of the day.

ABOVE LEFT: Teenager buys first car. Published in Life, *New York, May 26, 1958. Photographer: A. Y. Owen. Courtesy Time Inc.* ABOVE RIGHT: *Man in bell-bottom jeans at Woodstock Music Festival. 1969. Photographer: Burk Uzzle. Courtesy Archive Pictures Inc.* OPPOSITE: *Andy Warhol. Jeans by Wrangler; shirt by*

Western House. Fashion editorial published in L'Uomo Vogue, *Milan, June–July 1980. Photographer: Gilles Bensimon. Courtesy Edizioni Conde Nast S.p.A.*

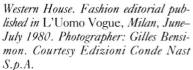

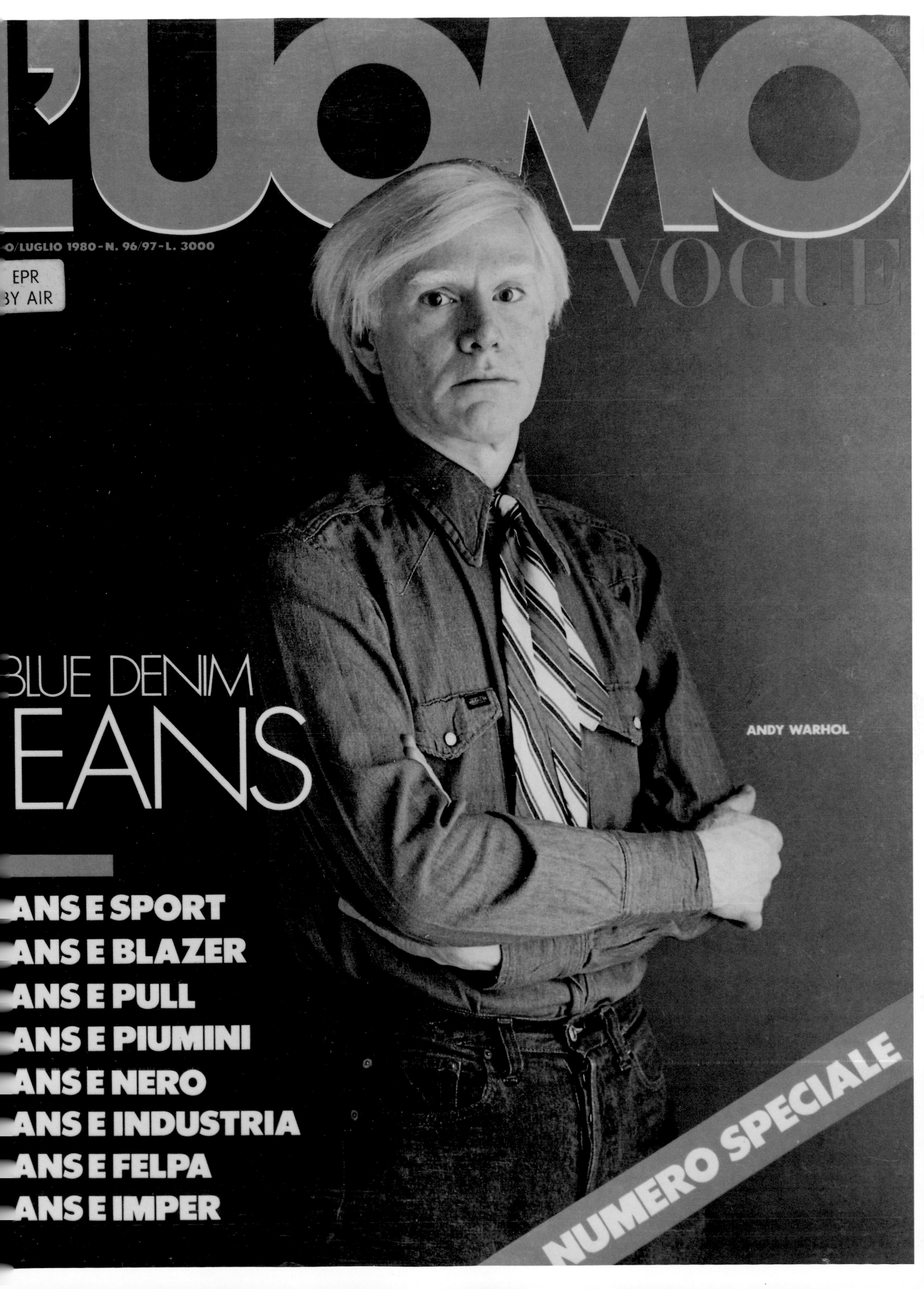

L'UOMO
VOGUE

O/LUGLIO 1980 - N. 96/97 - L. 3000

EPR
BY AIR

BLUE DENIM
EANS

ANDY WARHOL

ANS E SPORT
ANS E BLAZER
ANS E PULL
ANS E PIUMINI
ANS E NERO
ANS E INDUSTRIA
ANS E FELPA
ANS E IMPER

NUMERO SPECIALE

The T-shirt assumed a mythic role in the 1950s by means of movies and television. It emphasized Marlon Brando's brutish machismo, James Dean's air of the young renegade, and Art Carney's raffish lower-class style (in the way he slipped a vest over the shirt). By the 1980s, the T-shirt would be the dress of the artist, perennial juvenile and outsider. All were ameliorations of the initial understanding of the T-shirt symbol.

ABOVE: Marlon Brando as Stanley Kowalski in film version of A Streetcar Named Desire. *1951. Photographer: John Engstead for Warner Bros. Courtesy Kobal Collection and Staley-Wise Gallery. TOP RIGHT: Art Carney in "The Honey-*

mooners." c. 1955. Unknown photographer. Courtesy Viacom Enterprises. BOTTOM RIGHT: Artist Keith Haring wearing one of his own T-shirts. 1985. Photographer: Jeannette Barron. Courtesy Staley-Wise Gallery. OPPOSITE: James Dean in Rebel without a Cause. *1955. Unknown photographer for Warner Bros. Courtesy Kobal Collection.*

Born of proletarian utility, the white T-shirt made an easy shift to leisure in the 1950s. Moving from underwear to outerwear, the T-shirt was also transformed from lower to middle class.

TOP: *John and Jacqueline Kennedy in their Georgetown garden, Washington, D.C.*

c. 1956. Unknown photographer. CENTER: Actor David Neidorf. 1987. Photographer: Jeannette Barron. Courtesy Staley-Wise Gallery. BOTTOM: Truman Capote. 1947. Photographer: Henri Cartier-Bresson. Courtesy Magnum Photos, Inc.

college football team to reveal its identity, the T-shirt quickly becam the bearer of advertisements, ideas, and judgments. In 1973, *Women Wear Daily* declared: "The T-shirt is the year's number one counte culture status symbol." In 1975, some 48 million printed T-shirts we on the market in America, and like numbers were produced over th next several years. Production was, of course, artificially sustained the fact that sentiments often faded long before the T-shirts; one yea fad remark was soon passé. Writer Fran Lebowitz responded to the sh cacophony in the 1970s with the cynical remark: "If people don't wa to listen to you, what makes you think they want to hear from yo sweater?"

Pronouncements were made in symbols and in words. Wit on th chest was rampant. In 1975, Budweiser Beer launched advertising shirts in Florida and California during the spring vacations for colle students, whose status presumably rose as they return to campus wi proof of having been to the beach and having the supposed maturity drink beer. Artist Keith Haring wrote poignant and pointed messag in which graffiti as a committed visual language was combined wi moral judgments. The London designer Katharine Hamnett print dour statements on T-shirts, beginning in 1983, that constitute a histo chronicle of our time. Among the most controversial of her expressio was "59 percent say no to Pershing," a disarmament T-shirt that s wore to a reception at No. 10 Downing Street when Prime Minist Thatcher was present. If the T-shirt is the natural tabula rasa of clot ing, the statement T-shirt confirms the plausibility of clothing's ov messages and acknowledges that the garment is, at skin's surface a the external world's approach, an innate and eloquent sign system.

In the second half of the 1970s, logos and political views were s passed by trompe l'oeil T-shirts in fictive dress, in particular, an ill sionistic tuxedo shirt and jacket, which played with the difference b tween formal and informal dress. Subsequently, parts of the anator and whole bodies were revealed. The acknowledgment of Japane fashion in the West was adapted to the T-shirt through a vogue for Ja anese calligraphy—generally chosen for its form and not its meanin

The torn T-shirt, perhaps deriving from Brando's epic image in t screen version of *A Streetcar Named Desire* (1951) and stimulated by t punk style, was extended to sweatshirts in 1983 by the film *Flashdan* The repeated success of the television series "The Honeymoone (broadcast in the 1955–56 season but rerun many times over the yea is owing in no small measure to the appearance of Art Carney in the r of Ed Norton, the worker with pretensions to grandeur, who in mo propriety tops off a T-shirt with a vest.

What had once been an undershirt continues to play a compelling r for men. Although clothing manufacturers have repeatedly sought develop versions in color, the white T-shirt remains the more cruc item of dress. Revived in the 1980s because of its associations w youth and the 1950s, it served as advertising imagery for such design as Ralph Lauren and Calvin Klein. Both men wore the T-shirt in th own ads, the former dressed in jeans and drinking beer, the lat slouching, suggesting a 1950s tough, in his greased hair and rolled-sleeves alluding to "beefcake" imagery of the time. Calling forth t past of one generation and invoking the supposed history of the signer's life, the contemporary advertising of T-shirts acknowledg history in recapitulation.

THE REBEL

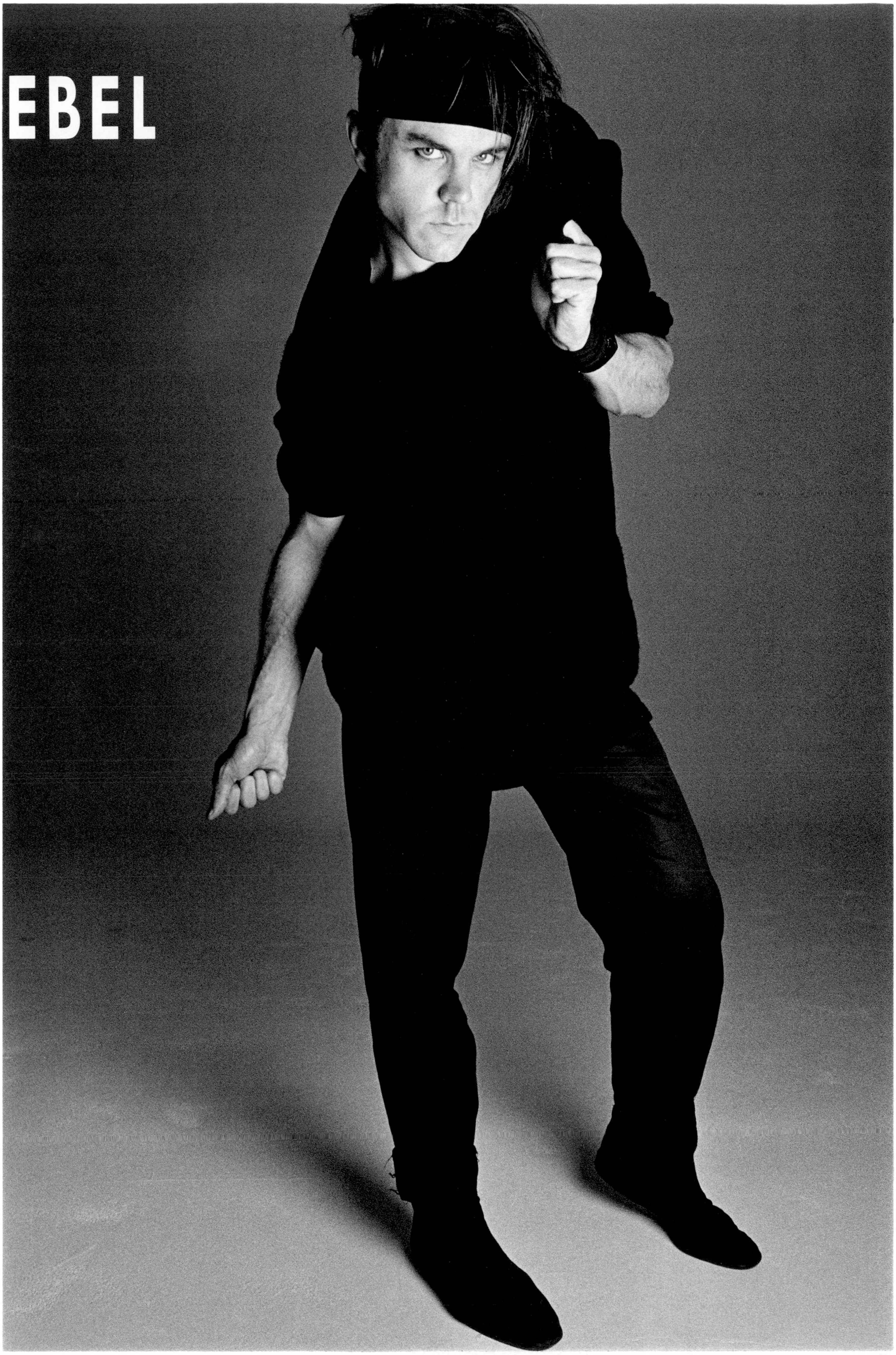

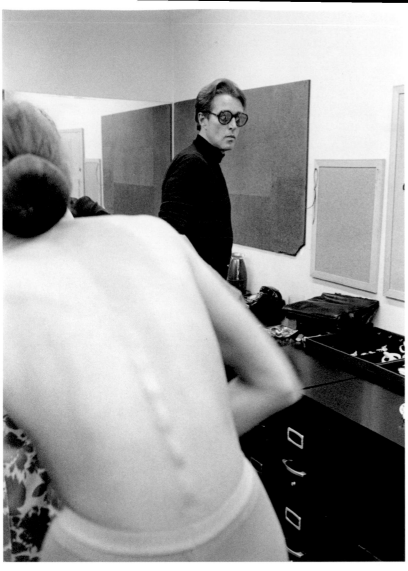

The rebel wears black. Whether he wears the leather jacket of the mo[torcycle] gang or the turtleneck of the beatnik, he wears black. The nineteenth-century romantic esteemed black, but the twentieth-cen[tury] man has found it sinister, isolated, and iniquitous. Black serves a[s] a sign of social militancy and provocation for men in a way that it doe[s] not for women. Although the little black dress is a costume of elegance for women, men in this century have worn gray or a limited palette o[f] colors in deliberate avoidance of black. When black enters the mal[e] wardrobe, it arrives with arresting authority and with a social goad When social activists of the 1960s and 1970s sought to represent thei[r] challenge to the social order, the confrontation was dressed in black Some chanted "Black Power," specifying racial equality, and the[ir] rhetoric was garbed in clothes that questioned authority and offered a[n] alternative power, the defiant puissance of black.

Their comrades in arms came from the netherworld of cyclists an[d] other phantoms of the night. Rock musicians readily appropriated th[e] imagery of black leather to affirm the outsider role of their music an[d] the "bad boy" character of their personas. To wear leather reinforce[d] the sense of the social dare that black had made. Artists, poets, and de[signers] have, of course, always worn black, establishing, thereby, a lin[k] to the dandy tradition. The dandy's subjective and subversive quar[rel] with the Establishment becomes the rebel's ostensible repudiation [of] the conventional. He deliberately stands outside the convention [of] dress by preferring black. Contemporary fashion designers Halston an[d] Stephen Sprouse wear black, the former from an ascetic and spiritu[al] reductivism, the latter from a rock-inflected rejection of facile soci[al] discourse. The artist's decision in dress is thus to create a metaphysic[al] difference from the mass of modern man, an equivalent to clerical dres[s]. When Julien Sorel in Stendhal's epic *The Red and the Black* (1831) [is] forced to choose his world, he must decide between the red of the m[il]itary and the black of the Church. Likewise, the black favored in th[e] 1980s by Japanese, British, and American fashion designers is a spiritu[al] black endowed with the secrets not only of faith but of isolation a[nd] separation from the things of this world. The gallery of men in black—musicians, writers, performers—wear their badges of priestly arts [in] manifest departure from the majority of men who avoid black in the[ir] wardrobe.

The men of shadows cast their presence in inky jeans and black shir[ts] but their preeminent form is the black-leather jacket. Assumed by t[he] motorcyclist in adaptation of the clothing worn by First World W[ar] aviators and cycle officers, the leather jacket became by the 1940[s a] symbol of the road warrior, a man in combat with all positive soc[ial] forces. In 1947, an onslaught of men on motorcycles would terroriz[e a] town: a true episode of a motorcycle gang invading a California to[wn] became the basis of *The Wild One* (1954), a film in which the gang lead[er] wears the black-leather jacket of civil threat. A decade later, a simi[lar] jacket would confirm the same renegade rejection of discipline and a[u]thority when Peter Fonda donned black leather for the film *The W[ild] Angels* (1966). The operative word is "wild" in both instances, alludi[ng] not only to the skin of the leather, but to the essence of the black-o[r] fitted men, who sign their defiance of civilization by wearing bla[ck]. Even more pacific men have worn black leather in its titillating a[nd] subversive role as the threat to social norms.

Claus von Bülow as photographed by Helmut Newton is a parado[x]ical man in black; he is a worldly prince of money and power in [a] leather jacket. As this figure stands before a fireplace, it is as if the r[en]egade had somehow stolen into the house of authority and the man [in] black, a dark angel, had taken dominion.

The rebel may offer insurrection by not conforming to dress rul[es] but he saves his supreme revolution for the seizure of the one color t[hat] men's fashion abjures in the twentieth century. The rebel is the m[an] in black.

Since the days of the beat generation in the 1950s, black knit has been the emblem of nihilism, even in the rarefied precincts of fashion design. It was adopted in the 1980s by two designers who are a generation apart, Halston, above, and Stephen Sprouse, preceding page, who perhaps wore it in the beat spirit. Sprouse also wears Christiaan's black-jersey headband, a high-style nod to sweatbands of the street.

PRECEDING PAGE: Designer Stephen Sprouse. 1983. Photographer: Francesco Scavullo. Courtesy the photographer. ABOVE: Designer Halston at work. 1977. Photographer: Barbra Walz. © *1989 Barbra Walz.*

In fashion, as in life, the rebel wears black. In this dialogue between two young fashion rebels, the man in the foreground is aggressively dressed in black leather, a contrast to the one in back, a stylized composition in black wool, his white socks mitigating the assertion of black. Although the skateboard modifies the message of the leather, the costume retains its tough-guy connotations and insolence.

OPPOSITE: Michael Schmidt and Lawrence C. 1985. Photographer: Isabel Snyder. Courtesy the photographer.

An actor and a musician join the harlequinade of men in black. Preferred by the outsider, black is antisocial and militant, a symbol of indifference and defiance.

ABOVE: Actor Julian Sands. 1987. Photographer: Josef Astor. Courtesy the photographer. BELOW: Musician John Lurie. c. 1982. Photographer: Jeannette Barron. Courtesy Staley-Wise Gallery.

...osters and rock singers are ever ...black. And the man in black in ...advertising image, above right, ...had, bad, and dangerous to ...ow.

...VE: Writer William Burroughs.
...4. Photographer: Jeannette Barron.
...rtesy Staley-Wise Gallery. RIGHT:
...sician Tom Waits. Published in The
...e, London, November 1985. Pho-
...apher: Steve Tynan. Courtesy the
...ographer. TOP RIGHT: Advertisement
...Guess? by Georges Marciano. 1987.
...tographer: Wayne Maser. Courtesy
...s? by Georges Marciano.

motorcycle gang in leather jack-
, opposite, stops for a roadside
pair. Such bands were commonly
nd on California highways in
1940s. In 1947, a wild, beer-
nking horde of motorcyclists on
rleys, including the man above,
aded the northern-California
vn of Hollister. From the devas-
on there developed a twen-
th-century mythos regarding
ing barbarians on wheels who
vel in packs and imperil civi-
d values. In *The Wild One*
54), a movie based on the
nt, the story takes form around
rlon Brando, at right, who leads
marauders in black leather.

*OSITE TOP: Roadside repair, Santa
ra County, California. April 5, 1940.
tographer: Rondal Partridge. Cour-
National Archives. ABOVE: Motor-
st in Hollister, California. Published
ife, New York, July 21, 1947. Pho-
apher: Barney Peterson. Courtesy
e Inc. RIGHT: Marlon Brando in
e Wild One. 1954. Unknown pho-
apher for Columbia Pictures. Courtesy
mann Archive.*

Cinematic apocalypses *The Wild
Angels* (1966), opposite, and *Mad
Max beyond Thunderdome* (1985),
left, revolve around social radicals
and life reduced to the primitive
impulse.

OPPOSITE: Peter Fonda in The Wild
Angels. *1966. Unknown photographer
for A.I.P. Courtesy Kobal Collection.
LEFT: Mel Gibson in* Mad Max beyond
Thunderdome. *1985. Unknown photographer for Warner Bros. Courtesy Kobal Collection.*

The four bikers above, photographed in 1965, are less awesome and menacing than some mythic figures in leather. Many of their gestures in clothing and jewelry, such as wearing a single earring, have been assimilated through punk into the style of the young.

TOP AND BOTTOM LEFT: Members of a Chicago motorcycle gang. 1965. Photographer: Danny Lyon. Courtesy Witkin Gallery.

Fashion develops the mythos of the rebel even further in offering a tattooed iconoclast in jeans and leather jacket. Poet Gerard Malanga, above, has, like the aristocrats of art and poetry Charles Baudelaire and Theophile Gautier, a decided preference for black. Outlaw and elegant, it is capable of poetic metamorphosis, like the butterfly Malanga wears on his leather jacket.

LEFT: Model in jacket by Robrik Pelle; jeans by Guess? by Georges Marciano. Fashion editorial published in L'Uomo Vogue, *Milan, November 1986. Photographer: Nadir. Courtesy Edizioni Conde Nast S.p.A. ABOVE: Gerard Malanga. 1973. Photographer: Francesco Scavullo. Courtesy the photographer.*

The black-leather jacket commands attention and respect. The dress of confrontation and power, it is the sign of the social outcast, politically engaged but socially estranged. Black Panthers find common costume with beat poets and rock musicians in the adversarial strategy of leather.

TOP AND CENTER LEFT: Black Panthers, New York. 1969. Photographer: Charles Harbutt. Courtesy Archive Pictures Inc. BOTTOM LEFT: Ensemble by Moschino. Published in L'Uomo Vogue, Milan, July–August 1987. Photographer: Noboru Morikawa. Courtesy Edizioni Conde Nast S.p.A.

The animal expressionism of the leather-clad figure at left is as benign as the demeanor of the style rebel in leather above.

LEFT: Jacket, pullover, and shoes by M. & F. Girbaud; long johns by Tout les Caleçons. Fashion editorial published in Vogue Hommes International, *Paris, Fall–Winter 1987–88. Photographer: Lord Snowdon. Courtesy Publications Condé Nast S.A. ABOVE: Andrew Brucker. c. 1987. Photographer: Josef Astor. Courtesy the photographer.*

On the following pages, film actor and bodybuilder Arnold Schwarzenegger recapitulates the 1950s in jeans, T-shirt, brush cut, and black leather; and the stylized savagery of animal skin creates a natural discordance in the refined environment of Claus von Bülow.

FOLLOWING PAGES, LEFT: Arnold Schwarzenegger. Published in Interview, *New York, October 1985. Photographer: Greg Gorman. © 1989 Greg Gorman. RIGHT: Claus von Bülow. 1985. Photographer: Helmut Newton. Courtesy the photographer.*

The late Sid Vicious, right, the British rock musician who joined the Sex Pistols as bass guitarist and lead singer in 1977, was the embodiment of punk in street fashion. A decade later French designer Jean-Paul Gaultier satirizes the punk style in the biker pants at left.

RIGHT: Sid Vicious of the Sex Pistols. 1976. Unknown photographer. Courtesy Michael Ochs Archive. LEFT: Biker pants by Jean-Paul Gaultier. Fashion editorial published in Per Lui, *Milan, September 1987. Photographer: Bico Stupakoff. Courtesy Edizioni Conde Nast S.p.A.*

The fictive West of films and advertising has its counterpart in scenes of actual cowboys observed in this century.

CENTER RIGHT: The boys of the LS Ranch, near Tascosa, Texas. 1900. Photographer: Erwin E. Smith. Courtesy Library of Congress. TOP LEFT: Cattleman and horse at auction, San Angelo, Texas. November 1939. Photographer: Russell Lee. Courtesy Library of Congress. CENTER LEFT: Rick Bates, YP Ranch, Tuscarora, Nevada. 1985. Photographer: Kurt Markus. Courtesy Staley-Wise Gallery. BOTTOM LEFT: Cattleman John Mutz, Moreno Valley, Colfax County, New Mexico. February 1943. Photographer: John Collier. Courtesy Library of Congress.

The COWBOY

One of the most significant fashion images of the twentieth century was set by the cowboy. Although Annie Oakley may have stolen Buffalo Bill's thunder and transferred the image across gender lines, the deep heart of the cowboy image is masculine. And whether that masculinity is putative or real, the image is compelling. The emotional components of the cowboy role are independence, rugged individualism, adaptability, and enjoyment of men's company. The cowboy is perceived as unchanging, living beyond fashion in a state of simplicity, day in day out, from morning until night. This "noble savage" of the range historically spent his days on horseback, herding cattle, surviving extremes of temperature and other difficult circumstances. Indeed, the classic image of the cowboy is based on the men who, in the crucial two or three decades after the close of the Civil War, made the long cattle drives along the Chisholm Trail, from San Antonio, Texas, across the Great Plains to market at Abilene, Kansas. They had been Confederate soldiers, many of them, unwilling to face the consequences of the War between the States. Or else they were adventurers, taking advantage of the great cattle boom that swept the country from 1863 to the closing years of the century. On those trips, the cowboy survived for weeks in one outfit, adding layers of clothing in cold weather, achieving an ad hoc style.

The cowboy in full regalia is prepared for anything. Starting from the round up, he wears high-heeled boots that are adapted to gripping the stirrups; his spurs, essential for moving a recalcitrant horse, give him armadillo-like invulnerability. His blue jeans are durable and his leather chaps protective, also like a natural armor. His large belt buckle is a badge of honor, perhaps won in rodeo competition; and his sturdy belt frees him from suspenders' constraints. His plaid flannel shirt is cool enough for arid sun and warm enough for Plains nights. His bandanna mops away the day's perspiration, dresses wounds, and shields him from the elements and the dust of the trail. His hat is both helmet and shield, in its many variations his most personal sign.

Romantic visions of the American cowboy turn on the spirit of adventurism and independence that flourished in the nineteenth century. He is presented as an American Adam, whose forthright, antiurbane lack of sophistication masks an unabashedly (but perhaps brutishly) honest man. His ancestors in style are the *vaquero* (the Mexican cowboy) and the Indian (whose horsemanship and self-reliance were legendary). Owen Wister's *The Virginian* (1902), one of the most popular

Among the characteristic items of cowboy dress are the bandanna, pearl-snap shirt, belt with large buckle, jeans, leather chaps, and boots. The contemporary cowboy, like his nineteenth-century ancestor, is manifestly self-sufficient and equipped to be the man for all seasons and circumstances.

ABOVE: Lloyd Sanders, Bell Ranch, New Mexico. 1985. Photographer: Kurt Markus. Courtesy Staley-Wise Gallery.

From left to right, trousers with sawtooth appliqué, a fringed, porcupine-quill vest, and a scalloped-bib prairie shirt are elaborations of cowboy dress that add a touch of theater to the image. Although silent-movie-star Tom Mix, left and far right, drifted from cowpunching to Wild West shows to movies, William Gibbs McAdoo, center, was a New York lawyer, a seeker after the nomination for President, and the son-in-law of President Woodrow Wilson: in short, his credentials as a cowboy are dubious. His elegant vest, however, is accompanied by a shirt with leather cuffs, standard gear for the rodeo cowboy in roping steers.

TOP LEFT: Silent-movie star Tom Mix and his horse Tony. c. 1925. Unknown photographer for Fox. Courtesy Library of Congress. TOP CENTER: William Gibbs McAdoo, center, presenting trophy to rodeo rider. c. 1928. Unknown photographer. Courtesy Library of Congress. TOP RIGHT: Tom Mix. c. 1922. Unknown photographer for Fox. Courtesy Library of Congress.

In 1940, Farm Security Administration photographer Russell Lee focused on the quintessential footwear of the cowboy, his boots with a slanted high heel worn with standard five-rowel spurs. The Texas shop window, bottom, photographed about the same date, contains an array of cowboy gear, presumably the vernacular wear of the San Angeleno patrons of the shop. In the portrait of a young cowboy from 1985, opposite, there is a rectitude and natural style, born of function, that is reminiscent of Renaissance portraiture.

RIGHT: Farmer's boots, Pie Town, New Mexico. June 1940. Photographer: Russell Lee. Courtesy Library of Congress. BOTTOM: Shop window, San Angelo, Texas. c. 1940. Unknown photographer. Courtesy Library of Congress. OPPOSITE: Tim McGinnes, LS Ranch, Monello, Nevada. 1985. Photographer: Kurt Markus. Courtesy Staley-Wise Gallery.

When Alan Ladd approached a bar in *Shane* (1953) and asked for a soda pop, he was ridiculed by the cowboys. In 1919, humorist Will Rogers, below, sidled up to the bar for a glass of milk, and perhaps made gentle fun of Prohibition, newly proclaimed the law of the land. The West was wild and hard drinking in one fiction, but in another, it was decent and wholesome. The homily spewing Rogers, who only a few years before had been spinning his lariat in the Ziegfield Follies, was perhaps articulating the cowboy ideal of a virtuous man.

BELOW: Will Rogers. c. 1919. Unknown

photographer. Courtesy Bettmann Archive.

Roy Rogers, opposite, added singing to the cowboy's rustic repertory. From 1935 to 1953 a singing cowboy in the movies, he became a television star of some magnitude in the 1950s, which provided the occasion for elaborate costumes, not the least of which were his trademark eagle-decorated boots.

OPPOSITE: Roy Rogers and his horse Trigger. c. 1950. Unknown photographer. Courtesy Kobal Collection.

novels of its day, gave the lure of the West a figure in the cowboy, al one whose roots were in the East. His posture on the Western hori was heroic, and his style has remained commanding.

Revivals of Western clothing have recurred in the present cent in the 1960s, under the Presidency of a Texan, Lyndon Baines Johns and as recently as the early 1980s, in the first flush of the Ronald Rea Presidency, whose ties with Texas were cinematic, not real. Yet W ern dress has always transcended the region and provided specific tions for mimicking the cowboy hero without adopting the full rega Depictions of late-nineteenth-century cowboys, beyond the artific rodeo riders and entertainment figures, suggest considerable adap use of clothing, in which apparel has been seized from more for contexts in a kind of improvisational style determined by availabi Thus, cowboys at a campfire early in the twentieth century sport v and band-collar shirts like those worn in formal dress, as well as bandannas and ten-gallon hats that are certifiably the gear of the boy. Many of the most rugged figures on the long cattle drives along Chisholm Trail were soldiers who had served in the Civil War and tled thereafter in the rich, expansive lands of Texas. Their clothing military and even Indian in origin, but it would be adopted by othe unique to the cowboy. Thus Theodore Roosevelt, who spent the y from 1883 to 1886 ranching in the Dakota Territory, wore fringe mannered adaptation of Indian decoration, but his cartridge belt bib-front buckskin shirt were appropriated from the Civil War vete who blazed a trail through the West.

From California came jeans, their adaptability proved by the m and readily appreciated by the cowboy. Not only were jeans esse for their narrow cut, their use of denim made them durable; and fabric was adopted for use in a jacket, in its rugged replacement of frock coat being not merely a jacket but a place of countless pockets if necessary, a sort of pillow, as well.

The bandanna, a modification of the Spaniard's scarf, was ofter most flamboyant aspect of the cowboy's wardrobe, especially when with an unexpected Plains panache. The knottings of broad sca make these neckerchiefs an important part of the cowboy's style, one that has seldom been adopted by the urban cowboy because near-dandy aspect. Once deprived of its function, the neckerchie tered the netherworld of neckties and was suppressed.

The cowboy's spurs, derived from the dandified *Chihuahuas*, th ver-inlaid implements worn by the *vaquero* and perhaps originatir the Mexican state by that name, were for the most part, a reduc version of this elaborate gear. Necessary to prod the horse but gene clumsy on the ground, the spurs of the American cowboy were sim fied, most often a five- or six-point rowel projected off the back of boot. The shank of the spur could be straight, half-dropped, drop gal-legged (in the form of a women's leg), or goosenecked, but simple, straight spur was most common. Thus, a working cowboy m prefer a five-point rowel on a straight shank worn over fancy boots decorative stitching. Rolled-up jeans complete the detail. Wes cowboys sometimes add the *frivole* of jingle bobs, metal pendants hang from the shank and sound as they hit each other, adding a wor music to riding and walking. Although the spur is necessary in ri (and its appearance in photography and films adds to the bristly pr of the cowboy hero), it has no purpose in any street adaptation of style.

The cowboy boot, a subject of fetish and fancy, was initially ge ated by necessity. The high, underslung heel, which came into b in the 1860s, facilitated riding as it gripped the stirrup but became a inconvenience on the ground. Creating an awkward imbalance or level surfaces, the underslung heel could, however, dig into the gro for leverage in roping cattle. The fancy boots with decorative stitc followed later in the nineteenth century as a manifestation of the manticized version of the cowboy.

Of like status is the cowboy hat, an item of apparel still favored visible sign of the old West, where it is even worn today with the b ness suit. Across the vast expanse of the West, hat styles varied with elements against which they were a protection: the Mexican-der

sombrero, with broad brim and high peak, served well in the windle[ss?] sun and heat of the Southwest; the low-crown hat of the Plainsman w[as?] a good guard against wind and rain. The Texas hat—the Hoss Ca[rt?]wright and Tom Mix hat, with the wide brim and high, pinched crow[n?] preferred by those noted movie cowboys—was perhaps the most co[m?]mon and most utilitarian cowboy hat. A Westerner could spot a stran[g?]er's hat and identify his ranch or region by the pinch of the crown or t[he?] flex of the brim.

The well-stocked window of a Western shop, photographed in 194[?] reveals laced-front shirts, boots, lariats, ten-gallon hats, and scarve[s?] suggesting the popularity of Western-style clothing. The extremes [of?] Western dress were reached not in what cowboys actually wore but [in?] the garb of entertainment figures—performers in the Wild West show[s?] early silent-movie stars, rodeo riders, even television performers. [A?] preference for exaggerated styles had little to do with the authentic ge[ar?] of the cowboy. Guns and holsters, not always necessary on the long tra[il?] became essential on the screen in a vision of the cowboy as moral e[x?]emplar. Silent-film stars Will Rogers, Tom Mix, Wild Bill Elliott, a[nd?] a host of others wore the full regalia of the cowboy hero, at times to t[he?] point of unlikelihood, wearing chaps indoors and dragging spurs on t[he?] ground. And those movie heroes adopted white or black hats, depen[d?]ing on their "good guy" or "bad guy" roles. By the time an affable, i[n?]fluential singing cowboy named Roy Rogers (originally an actor nam[ed?] Leonard Slye) came along, the fancy outfitting of the cowboy hero h[ad?] become a matter of great style but little authenticity. Rogers, who[se?] film career had begun in 1935, achieved great success on television [in?] the 1950s. In that era, his trademarks were eagle-decorated Texas bo[ots?] and a shirt with fringed yoke, piped pockets, and pearl-capped sn[ap?] closings—a fine example of a Western shirt from the dude's vanta[ge?] point. Rogers's horse Trigger was likewise dressed to the nines.

Boots were a signature style for many cowboys and continue to be [to?]day. Decorative variations such as contrasting materials and colo[rs?] piped edgings, inlays, appliqué, and clustered and color-modula[ted?] topstitching have been expanded by designers such as Lucchese, To[ny?] Lama, Justin, and Nacona, who enjoy a wealthy, committed, and [in?]ternational clientele for custom-fitted boots. Standard models, such [as?] those made by Frye, reach a wider audience at a more modest range [of?] prices.

John Wayne, no stranger to Western dress, not only played cowb[oy?] roles but also took on the part of a woodsman and pioneer. In *The Fight[ing?] Kentuckian* (1949), his role called for a fringed buckskin shirt and si[de?]laced pants, along with the pioneer's coonskin cap. Thirty years lat[er?] the men's fashion magazine *Gentleman's Quarterly*, influenced in eq[ual?] parts by a serious return to nature and a love of more ostentatious d[ec?]oration, created an amalgam of the pioneer and the cowboy, outfitt[ing?] him in a suit of buckskin with lacing defining the outer seams of t[he?] pants and their fly, and suede fringe giving flamboyance to the jack[et?] The conflation of pioneer and cowboy was a most sympathetic one[.?]

The film hero Shane, whose only vice was soda pop, was likew[ise?] outfitted in buckskin, for its natural lightness of color, its authentici[ty?] and its softness of line. *Shane* (1953) is based on a polar view of [the?] American West: the hero was a figure of purity and rustic simplici[ty?] dressed in garments made of rich natural materials, whereas the villa[in?] who wore store-bought clothes, represented the vilifying land intere[sts?] that threatened the free culture of the Plains. Shane had impresse[d a?] generation of children in the 1950s with the pastoral honesty of [his?] fringe, and twenty years later some of those children would wear frin[ge?] as a Western, American, and dandy motif, including a figure in a leat[her?] Captain America suit, now given pioneer heritage by long tassels [of?] fringe. Likewise, fringe would sprout again in the 1980s, on a leat[her?] jacket with metal studs, suggesting an elision of the Indian with [the?] cowboy and pioneer motifs. Clearly of a mixed past, the skin fringes [are?] an aberration in men's attire but provide a recurring opportunity [for?] adornment, sanctioned by their frontier history. The romantic as[so?]ciations of buckskin with the West make it appealing for men's cas[ual?] dress, as in the loose overshirt worn by actor Gary Cooper in a stu[dio?] photograph of 1930. His garb not only alludes to a Western motif [but?]

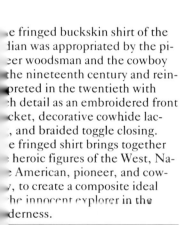

e fringed buckskin shirt of the lian was appropriated by the pi- er woodsman and the cowboy the nineteenth century and rein- preted in the twentieth with h detail as an embroidered front cket, decorative cowhide lac- , and braided toggle closing. e fringed shirt brings together heroic figures of the West, Na- American, pioneer, and cow- , to create a composite ideal he innocent explorer in the derness.

From its raw origin in sueded buckskin, the fringed shirt has been further reinterpreted in polychromed and black leather.

OSITE TOP: Theodore Roosevelt in the dlands of North Dakota. c. 1884. tographer: T. W. Ingersoll. Courtesy rary of Congress. OPPOSITE CENTER: n Wayne in The Fighting Ken- kian. *1949. Unknown photographer Republic Studios. Courtesy Kobal lection. OPPOSITE BOTTOM: Movie r Bill Elliott. c. 1933. Unknown tographer. Courtesy Library of Con- s.*

ABOVE LEFT: *Larry Piller, Los Angeles musician and tennis teacher, wearing a polychromed-leather Captain America suit. Fashion editorial published in* Life, *New York, September 25, 1970. Photog- rapher: Enrico Sarsini. Courtesy the photographer.* ABOVE: *Big Mike at Cooper Union. 1988. Photographer Tom Mc- Bride. Courtesy the photographer.*

**Come to where the flavor is.
Come to Marlboro Country.**

Marlboro Red or Longhorn 100's—
you get a lot to like.

Kings: 16 mg ''tar,'' 1.1 mg. nicotine—
100's: 17 mg ''tar,'' 1.1 mg. nicotine av. per cigarette, FTC Report Oct.'74

Warning: The Surgeon General Has Determined
That Cigarette Smoking Is Dangerous to Your Health.

Marlboro

also accommodates the open-collared shirt beneath in accordance wit
contemporary dress.

Of all the movie cowboys who commanded a loyal following, perhap
none were more consistently persuasive than Gary Cooper and John
Wayne, both strongly identified with men's Western clothing. In *Th
Westerner* (1940), Cooper wore a suede jacket over a blue-check shir
with a yellow bandanna, a long-trail improvisation of mixed materials
In *High Noon* (1952), he was dressed in pin-striped trousers and vest wit
shawl collar befitting his role as Marshal Will Kane. He wore the trap
pings of authority and power, with a watch chain stretched across hi
vest, string tie, white shirt, and marshal's badge. If his clothing seeme
to have been sent out from the East, his imagery was also complicate
by his wearing a black hat, ending the simplest fashion distinction be
tween good and evil in the old West. John Wayne's striding Wester
presence was marked by leather vests, bib-front shirts, buckskin, and

Since the 1950s, the American
West has been "Marlboro Country," and the cowboy has been the
"Marlboro Man," in an intense
identification of a brand of cigarettes with the cowboy. Leo Bur-
nett created the advertising campaign, making "an obscure brand
the biggest-selling cigarette in the
world," according to advertising
executive David Ogilvy. The campaign was so pervasive that Marlboro became an international mail-
order vendor of men's Western
wear featured in the ads.

Movie actor Gary Cooper was ph
tographed by Cecil Beaton wear
fringe, above, in 1930, a year aft
the release of his first all-talking
film, *The Virginian*, a version of t
successful Owen Wister novel,
which had been largely responsi
for shaping the myth of the cowl
in this century. Cooper would pl
cowboy roles in numerous films,
including *The Westerner* (1940), o
posite, in which he would seem
be the precursor of the Marlbor
Man.

*TOP LEFT: The Marlboro Man—Slicker
Gaze. 1975. Advertisement. Unknown
photographer. Courtesy Philip Morris
Incorporated. BOTTOM LEFT: The Marlboro Man—J. D. Saddle. 1971. Advertisement. Unknown photographer. Courtesy Philip Morris Incorporated.*

*ABOVE: Gary Cooper. 1930. Photog
pher: Cecil Beaton. Courtesy Sothel
London. OPPOSITE: Gary Cooper in
Westerner. 1940. Unknown photog
pher for Goldwyn-United Artists. Cou
Kobal Collection.*

ning: The Surgeon General Has Determined

Gary Cooper's performance as Marshal Will Kane, left, in *High Noon* (1952) transformed the handsome leading man into a mature actor with deep personal identification with his part. According to William K. Everson, writing in *The Western* (1962), Cooper's attire, unconventional in being black, conveyed the message that he was "a man of obvious destiny, force, and leadership."

LEFT: Gary Cooper in High Noon. *1952. Unknown photographer for United Artists. Courtesy The Museum of Modern Art Film Stills Archive.*

John Wayne, below, received an Oscar for his characterization of the sympathetic old cowboy Rooster Cogburn in *True Grit* (1969). "In a career that spanned almost fifty years," wrote his biographer Tom Tierney, "John Wayne became the quintessential Western star and eventually a prototype of the American hero." His first leading role in a Western was in *The Big Trail* (1930), and he would play in scores of others over the next four decades. In his last film, *The Shootist* (1976), he again played an aging gunslinger, a role resembling his own struggle with cancer at the time. Wayne died in 1979.

BELOW LEFT: John Wayne in True Grit. *1969. Unknown photographer for Paramount Pictures. Courtesy Kobal Collection.*

A long raincoat that conjures up the range and the functional protection of the cowboy, opposite, has been preserved in Western gear, maintained in marketing, and renewed through its inspiration to European designer Giorgio Armani, right. A clothing company advertising in *The New Yorker* in the 1980s claimed of its version of this coat: "Classic horseman's duster protects you, your rump, your saddle, and your legs down to the ankles. Because it's cut very long to do the job, it's unintentionally very flattering. With or without a horse." Perhaps the most convincing word in this advertisement is "unintentional," suggesting that a handsome appearance is achieved not by design but by discovering the functionally fortuitous.

ABOVE RIGHT: Duster by Giorgio Armani. Fashion editorial published in Mondo Uomo, *Milan, September 1987. Photographer: Aldo Fallai. Courtesy the photographer. OPPOSITE: Michigan cowboy in duster. 1987. Published in* Detroit Monthly, *June 1987. Photographer: Monte Nagler. Courtesy the photographer.*

surprisingly, bandanna flair, an unlikely touch in light of the actor's straightforward masculine image.

Yet, if the bandanna was a trace of style for the movie cowboy, it would figure as well in modern advertising addressed to men. Convening the imagery of freedom, hard work, and style, Marlboro cigarettes created an advertising campaign centered on "Marlboro Country," a place that is the American West at its most desirable. In a long succession of advertisements dating from the early 1970s, an evocation of the Chisholm Trail wardrobe, including chaps, long raincoats, jeans, plaid shirts, and leather vests, has been called upon to symbolize a country of freedom and contentment.

Enthusiasm for the American West is a phenomenon that has spread beyond the United States, taking on an international dimension in large part through the dissemination of American movies and television. The two media have endorsed the mythology of the Western frontier as enthrallingly as did James Fenimore Cooper's *Leatherstocking Tales* a cen-

In mid-century the cowboy role was realized in the heroic idealism of Shane, the paragon of plain and Plains virtue, but in the closing years of the century there would emerge the glamorous midnight cowboy, the gambler, entrepreneur, and tycoon, the high-flying maverick whose boots are hand-tooled and who appropriates his evening attire from the man about town.

LEFT: Alan Ladd in Shane. *1953. Unknown photographer for Paramount Pictures. Courtesy Kobal Collection. ABOVE AND BELOW RIGHT: Above, appliquéd and leather-fringed jacket and pants by Debbie Klein; lariat by Nick Philolius. Below, suede shirt for Char Designs by Char and Cher; bandanna by Lugini; silver-buckled belt by Barry Kieselstein-Cord; hat by North Beach Leather; silver-tipped bolo by Sunset Trains; boots by Nacona; spur strap by Nick Philolius; spurs by Vogt. Fashion editorial published in* GQ, *August 1979. Photographer: Albert Watson. Courtesy the photographer. OPPOSITE: Actor Tom Selleck for Chaz Cologne. 1979. Advertisement. Photographer: Claude Mougin. Courtesy Chaz Cologne for Men / Revlon.*

tury ago, when generations of Europeans were entranced by the adventure of a new land and its pioneers. Italian designer Giorgio Armani, for example, appropriated the long, oversized raincoat of the cowboy in a design that rivals the versions continuously present in America through dealers in riding and Western clothes. To be sure, long after the West was won, the world is one, and international fashion, with its nexus in urban style, continues to employ the imagery of the cowboy. If readers of fashion magazines have wandered from the trail to cities, fashion has followed them as tenaciously as any posse. *Gentleman's Quarterly* announced in August 1979: "The cowboy look comes to town," and posed an elegantly clad urban cowboy in relief against a twentieth-century glass tower, as another, in half-length portrait, clutched his meticulously tooled boot like an icon. The urban cowboy was given a new opportunity to wear the dress of the West but to figure in the contemporary city. In the same period, Chaz, a Revlon fragrance, featured the actor Tom Selleck in an advertisement associating its col-

ogne with a modified and urbanized Western style that included Western boots and hat with black tie.

The cowboy on the long trail would have had little affinity with his modern image. Even as big-city and international appropriations have represented him in a very different way, the cowboy yet remains. The style, even in his own time, was one of units and increments—it was adaptive. Thus, a contemporary urban figure in bolo tie and studded leather as concha belt has as much of an American flavor as any cowboy, but he also partakes of an internationalism that has assimilated and immortalized him.

The highly dandified urban cowboy, opposite, takes part in the myth of West, but his role is that hustler, gambler, and ladies' man rather than the man of probity and innocent perfection.

OPPOSITE: Fashion portrait. 198
Photographer: Josef Astor. Courtesy
photographer.

The hippie often affected the cowboy style in the 1970s, drawing upon the myth of the cowboy as a renegade among renegades, ever on the outer edge of civilization.

ABOVE: Young hippie, New York City.
c. 1972. Photographer: Charles Gatewood. Courtesy Magnum Photos, Inc.
ABOVE RIGHT: Actor Dennis Hopper. c.
1970. Photographer: Dennis Stock.
Courtesy Magnum Photos, Inc.

The most popular military garment of our time may well be the trench coat. Originally designed for British officers , in England, it was a waterproof coat with woolen lining worn in the trenches of the First World War. Adapted for rainwear after the war, it rose to romantic heights through its association with men of the world such as the Prince of Wales and the film adventurers played by Joel McCrea and Humphrey Bogart.

ABOVE: *Edward, Prince of Wales, in Canada. c. 1925. Unknown photographer. Courtesy Bettmann Archive.* RIGHT: *Joel McCrea in* Foreign Correspondent. *1940. Unknown photographer for*

United Artists. OPPOSITE: *Dooley Wilson and Humphrey Bogart in* Casablanca. *1942. Unknown photographer for Warner Bros. Courtesy Kobal Collection.*

MILITARY MAN

he military man is the hero as warrior and guardian. In modern times
e is not only a combat warrior, but also a technological hero who has
on his victory through conquering the most advanced equipment of
arfare. His clothes have been custom designed if not custom made.
he wardrobe of parade dress has the greatest elan for the military man,
t it is the clothing of combat that makes its way back to civilian life.
Since war began, men have returned home from battle with new skills
d new insights developed in the course of combat. Materially, the
merican soldier has returned with such clothing as olive drabs, officers'
ats, Eisenhower jackets, pea coats, and aviator jackets and glasses.
all the military garments that have been adopted by the public for
ily use, however, the most dashing may be the trench coat. In name
efers to the trenches of the First World War, where it was the official
parel of British officers. Similar coats had been available earlier
rough such London-based tailors as Aquascutum and T. Burberry and
ns, but the codification of the trench coat came with the govern-

According to fashion historian John Berendt, General Dwight D. Eisenhower, Supreme Commander of Allied Forces in the Second World War, wore five different versions of the Eisenhower jacket. In the one at left, the fitted, waist-length jacket with ample sleeves and buttoned cuffs gives the General a trim yet somewhat informal appearance as he talks to men in battle dress. In a 1980s fashion derivation, bottom, the raised collar and casual pose diminish the military look of the garment.

TOP: General Eisenhower with combat troops on the eve of D-Day. June 1944. Unknown photographer. Courtesy Library of Congress. BOTTOM: Promotional brochure for Bill Robinson. Photographer: Steven Meisel. Courtesy Keeble Cavaco & Duka.

In 1968, a young Black Panther in fatigue jacket stands ready to wage a battle in defense of the poor, and in 1978, the movie director Milos Forman in like costume prepares to stage a film in the manner of a military campaign. Both roles imply battle mastery, and both men employ battle dress. A favorite neologism of the 1960s was "co-opt," the subverting of strong dissonant voices through their assimilation into the Establishment. In a sense, the seizing of military clothing in an antimilitary era was concomitantly an Establishment and a disestablishment action.

TOP LEFT: *Black Panther taking part in the Poor People's Campaign, Washington, D.C. 1968. Photographer: Jill Freedman. Courtesy Archive Pictures Inc.* TOP RIGHT: *Milos Forman, left, directing film version of* Hair. *1978. Photographer: Mary Ellen Mark. Courtesy Archive Pictures Inc.*

Camouflage clothing serves the military man as a survival strategy and form of disguise, but its association with the macho activity of the independent hero, such as the type portrayed in films by Arnold Schwarzenegger, right, has transferred its use to leisure wear.

ABOVE: *West Point cadets. 1987. Photographer: Marcia Lippman. Courtesy the photographer.* RIGHT: *Arnold Schwarzenegger in* Predator. *1987. Photographer: Zade Rosenthal for Twentieth Century Fox. Courtesy Kobal Collection.* LEFT: *Young man in camouflage. 1988. Photographer: Ellen Shanley.*

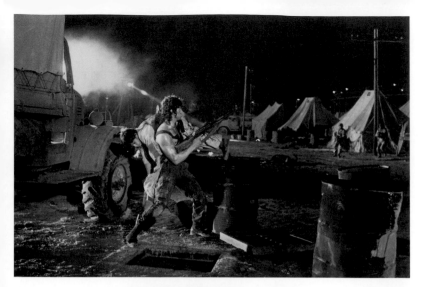

Rambo, a film character of the 1980s, a figure ever impervious to assault and pain, proved in successive incarnations that one man could constitute an army. In designer Franco Moschino's view, Rambo is a figure of raw but stylish masculinity—an armchair adventurer as soldier of fortune.

TOP: Sylvester Stallone stars in Rambo III. *1988. Photographer: Yoni Hamenachem. Courtesy Tri-Star Pictures, Inc. BOTTOM: Ensemble by Moschino. Fashion editorial published in men's edition of* Italian Design Fashion, *Florence, 1988–89. Photographer: Pierre Schwab. Courtesy Toscoeditrice.*

ment's specifications for the coats of British officers. The raincoat ac cepted as official dress is fundamentally the coat we know today– double-breasted, with epaulets, wrist straps that can be tightened t keep cold and wetness out, a large collar with throat latch, reinforce belt with D-rings, and a shoulder flap and back yoke for added prote tion. The cloth is water-resistant, dense, cotton khaki. Although th American man now views the trench coat as a kind of uniform, at its o igin it was almost an antiuniform. The late nineteenth-century wars Empire had demonstrated that full-dress outfitting hardly served th cause of victory; by the time of the First World War, the military of a nations had reserved full dress for parades and special events, instea creating a highly functional and purposefully unobtrusive garb for dai wear by both officers and enlisted men. The new demand for comfo and adaptability in military dress meant that the inventions of the mi itary could easily shift to civilian life after the war. To be sure, milita dress had always been of interest to the civilian, whether it be th transfer of tailors from military supply to the workrooms of daily life the adaptation of the tartan kilt of the Scottish warrior to the conve tional dress of men, women, and children. But the twentieth-centu insistence upon effectiveness in military dress made the transition civilian life even smoother.

The trench coat, called upon to withstand the mud and cold of E ropean trench warfare, is resonant with the elegiac overtones of the Fir World War, which invented a century in a massacre of innocents. Th coat returned to military service in the Second World War, where th American military also adopted it (in olive drab, not khaki). Betwee the wars, it flourished in civilian life, and it was worn by the Prince Wales and by movie heroes such as Joel McCrea, who played, in Alfr Hitchcock's *Foreign Correspondent* (1940), a journalist impressed in international espionage ever dressed in a trench coat. The D-ring originally intended for grenades, suggest the complete readiness of t modern swashbuckler. In an almost inexplicable combination meanings and implications, the trench coat has served not so much a uniform as a sign of the individualist, the intrepid journalist, and t internationalist-lover, all appearing in an appropriation from a unifor In *Casablanca* (1942), Humphrey Bogart provided the definitive he in a trench coat, the garment then having made a complete shift fro military life to the civilian. It has since come to be identified with go taste, but with romantic overtones derived from the writers, artists, a individualists associated with it. Defying the convention of the wo overcoat, some men have insisted on wearing the trench coat as standa outer wear, not waiting for rain to justify the versatile and quixotic c of the visionary as well as the officer in the trenches.

The intense documentation of the Second World War in photograp and film encouraged the appropriation of military clothing by civilia Camouflage suits, netted helmets, and khaki jackets from the Paci theater and the War in Europe were highly visible through such vehic as *Life Magazine* and movie newsreels. Even as the long war reached conclusion, the imagery of the hero was steadfast, and a triumph five-star general named Dwight D. Eisenhower came home with jacket. Eisenhower jackets (with the official military designation "w field jacket, M-1944") were first issued in November 1944 to troops Europe and North Africa, but the Eisenhower (so named because not only wore the jacket by preference but had commissioned t quartermaster to create the design in emulation of the one favored Field Marshal Montgomery, his British counterpart) came home at war's conclusion as a neat jacket with tight waist and broad should and chest, in a variety of durable materials. In subsequent years m American designers of sportswear for men have created versions of Eisenhower jacket, most far removed from the battlefield in th stylistic nuances yet honoring the romantic origin of the jacket.

Military surplus and the most pedestrian item of the military wa robe came to have a strong influence on civilian dress. The green fatig jacket was an element of the service uniform introduced in 1943 consisted of a moderately long jacket with drawstring waist and de patch pockets on the chest and flap-entry versions on the hips. It came available to the civilian population in the 1970s, chiefly throu

he conquest of the skies is one of
e great achievements of the
entieth century. The quiet cha-
ma of Charles Lindbergh and
e magnificence of his first soli-
y transatlantic flight in 1927 at-
cted a cult that extended to
ery aspect of his life. Men across
e country emulated his dress,
en the simple but elegant suede
ket in which he was photo-
aphed after his flight.

*HT: Aviator Charles A. Lindbergh in
nt of* The Spirit of St. Louis.
*927. Photographer: Underwood and
derwood. Courtesy Library of Con-
ss.*

e shearling jacket, its principle
-old, was adopted for high-alti-
e flying by the military before
Second World War.

*OSITE TOP: Flying Sergeant in high-
tude, cold-weather jacket, Lake Mu-
California. 1942. Photographer:
sell Lee. Courtesy Library of Congress.*

Gary Cooper, as Robert Jordan in
the film *For Whom the Bell Tolls*
(1943), wears the shearling jacket
of the Second World War flyer. Jordan undergoes a metamorphosis in
the story from American teacher to
Loyalist guerilla in Spain, his
transformation becoming evident
in clothing that makes a hero out of
the common man.

OPPOSITE BOTTOM: Gary Cooper in For
Whom the Bell Tolls. *1943. Unknown
photographer for Paramount Pictures.
Courtesy Kobal Collection.*

e aviator was pressed into mil-
duty, he became flyer and
bardier in one. The jacket,
net, and goggles of the three
er pilots above are repeated in
costumes of Gregory Peck,
plays the role of a bomber-
dron leader in the Second
d War, and Robert Redford,
aldo Pepper, a veteran of the
World War who goes to Hol-
od as a stunt man.

*E: Lt. Commanders J. H. Camp-
fighting leader; A. C. Masek, tor-
bombing wing; and De W. C. Wat-
scout. c. 1942. Photographer:
rwood and Underwood. Courtesy
ann Archive. TOP RIGHT: Gregory
in Twelve O'Clock High. Pub-
in Life, New York, February 20,
. Photographer: W. Eugene Smith.
tesy Time Inc. BOTTOM RIGHT:*

Robert Redford in The Great Waldo
Pepper. *1975. Unknown photographer
for Universal Pictures. Courtesy Kobal
Collection.*

its sale at Army-Navy stores. The fatigue jacket was often associa
with militant antiestablishment groups whose ideals were antitheti
to those of war-making. In a similar situation, camouflage had come i
use with a reversible twill coverall issued in the Pacific theater in 19
Used extensively throughout the war, it was joined by a two-piece j
gle-green camouflage suit that became available in March 1944. Ca
ouflage represented the valor of men who had survived the fierce jur
fighting of the war in the Pacific. Although camouflage clothing
worn by the United States military in Normandy in 1944, it was s
withdrawn when the pattern was mistaken by American troops for
German SS camouflage introduced earlier in the same year.

Returned to the United States, camouflage played a role in the ca
dress of soldiers, soldiers of fortune, and would-be military men. E
the young men of West Point wear T-shirts in camouflage patte
(1987), linking the postwar military to its history of jungle combat
suggesting the full-scale transference of military attitudes and ob
tives from the great battles to the doughty daredevilry of indivi
fighters. Thus, in the sustained uses of actors Arnold Schwarzeneg
in *Predator* (1987) and Sylvester Stallone in a succession of *Ra*
movies, camouflage is, like the trench coat some fifty years bef
transferred to the iconoclast and individual warrior from the ma
of collective good suggested in warfare. If big battles are thus
dividual accomplishments, the military connotation of clothing is
given to the solo fighter.

Foot soldiers have long contributed to the imaginative appropriat
of clothing, but the completely new image of the twentieth centu
the aviator. Seizing heaven, the pilot of the plane navigates the
horizon of the skies. The earliest flying aces were, of course, civil
Charles Lindbergh, who made the first solo transatlantic flight, is
tographed in characteristic dress: a soft jacket taken from casual
but otherwise not specific to the skies. Lindbergh, the innocently
onair flyer—a mythic Icarus of successful flight—was installed in
popular imagination along with the military aviator who, for the
ments and for new altitudes, required a leather jacket. The new h
the helmeted and goggled flyer, would create an enthralling im
through retrograde conventions. With soft helmet, leather gloves,
leather jacket, he was a recreation of the medieval knight in battle d
The barnstorming pilots of the years between the wars were darede
who expressed the romance of their profession. A movie called *The G
Waldo Pepper* (1975) cast Robert Redford in just such gallantry an
the knighthood of the sky. During the Second World War, con
brought serious challenge to the clothing of airmen: long-distance h
altitude flying cost many flyers their lives in frostbite, and the shear
jacket was the best protection against severe weather. B-7 goggles
troduced by the Air Force in 1933, were the standard issue, featu
rubber cushions on each half of the frame as a means of fixing the
in position before the eye. The courage of military aviators bec
legendary for the war years and thereafter, and such movie hero
Gregory Peck have exemplified the glamorous aviator.

The leather jacket of the aviator is subject to many modifications.
serves the adventuring image of the male. Work clothing is comb
with leather jackets for vernacular heroism in men photographe
Michael Disfarmer, and the leather jacket is worn as casual clothin
a young artist. To be sure, there are some items of military apparel
never cross over to civilian property, but the twentieth-century mil
has provided garments from olive-drab T-shirts to officers' great
that have lived a vital civilian life after their introduction by the mili
Stories of men stealing government-issue bomber jackets, preser
military khakis for their durability, and buying military surplus clot
are testimony to the battleworn as capable of peaceful use.

Among Michael Disfarmer's war-time portraits of the young men in his Arkansas town were two heroes in leather, the one at the left in aviator jacket. By the 1980s, even the new aviator jacket would be abraded or distressed, as with the one opposite. It is worn by a man too young to have known the jacket in its first incarnation but with an ideal of its use.

ABOVE: Small-town heroes in leather jackets. c. 1942. Photographer: Michael Disfarmer. Courtesy Staley-Wise Gallery. OPPOSITE: Painter Alberto Grieve. 1987. Photographer: Jeannette Barron. Courtesy Staley-Wise Gallery.

Whether in Africa or on the Western prairie, the hunter is an adventurer in search of big game. The popularity of the safari jacket, the garment most closely associated with big-game hunting, can be ascribed as much to its upper-class associations as to its true sporting use. The aristocratic origins of the hunting safari brought visibility along with class affiliation to the garment.

TOP: Director John Huston on set of The Misfits. *1960. Photographer: Eve Arnold. Courtesy Magnum Photos, Inc. CENTER: Mr. and Mrs. Ernest I. King of Winona, Minnesota, in Mombasa, Kenya. May 25, 1925. Unknown photographer. Courtesy Bettmann Archive. BOTTOM: Ava Gardner, Clark Gable, and Grace Kelly in* Mogambo. *1953. Unknown photographer for MGM. Courtesy Kobal Collection.*

"The great African safaris lasted for one century. From 1836 until 1939 unique conditions and eccentric individuals created a style of adventure that can never exist again. Abundant big game, ungoverned landscapes, suitable weapons, the lifelong habit of hunting, a zest for discovery and an appreciation of both hardship and luxury, all came together then in the vast bush of south-eastern Africa." —Bartle Bull, *Safari: A Chronicle of Adventure*, 1988

The adventurer stalks his quarry under many circumstances and in varied attire, but the hunter of big game stalks empire. Americans in particular, never having known empire, perhaps sought the semblances of it in the safari. Their fascination with the elaborate sporting expedition to Africa may have begun with the romantic novels of H. Rider Haggard, with his *King Solomon's Mines* and *Allan Quatermain* (both of 1885), and with the two-month safari of President Theodore Roosevelt in 1909, when he set out for Kenya to shoot game and to collect specimens for the Smithsonian Institution and the American Museum of Natural History. The outfitting of Roosevelt's ambitious expedition, the largest Africa had then known, was many months in preparation. The logistics of the trip were planned by a firm in Nairobi, but Roosevelt commissioned his hunting apparel from Abercrombie & Fitch Co., the New York "Outfitters to Sportsmen."

Ernest Hemingway also popularized the safari and its outfittings in America, not so much through his short story "The Short Happy Life of Francis Macomber" (published in *Cosmopolitan* Magazine in 1936), as in the subsequent film, *The Macomber Affair* (1947), starring Gregory Peck as the white hunter Robert Wilson and Robert Preston as Macomber. The white hunter as a fictional character is based on Haggard's Allan Quatermain—the English gentlemen hunter who is both inspiration and guide. Hemingway himself had made his first African safari in 1933–34, a ten-week affair for which he too commissioned a bush jacket from Abercrombie & Fitch; stock no. 476, it featured such devices as bellows pockets, cartridge loops ("where the breast pockets would have been," as he noted in his description of Wilson's clothes), and a pocket on the sleeve to hold a pack of cigarettes. Even without this jacket, the hunter that Hemingway was and the one that Robert

film *Out of Africa* (1985) pro-
d examples of hunting cloth-
for both men and women and
costume-designer Milena
onero one of the movie's seven
rs.

E: Robert Redford in Out of Africa.
5. *Unknown photographer for Uni-*
al Pictures. Courtesy M.C.A., Inc.

Yves Saint Laurent's interpretation of the safari shirt combined traditional bellows pockets with exposed lacing across the chest, creating a bravura statement antithetical to the chaste message of the undecorated safari shirt. Paramilitary modifications such as the drawstring waist gave the ever-serviceable safari jacket an even more adventuresome cast, heightened when worn slogging through fetid waters in a fashion editorial.

RIGHT: Paul Stooshnoff, Canadian movie director, wearing Yves Saint Laurent safari shirt. Fashion editorial published in Life, *New York, September 25, 1970. Photographer: Enrico Sarsini. Courtesy the photographer. BELOW: Survival jacket, safari jacket, shirt, and shorts by Gerani Themen. Fashion editorial published in* L'Uomo Vogue, *Milan, January 1987. Photographer: Lance Staedler. Courtesy Edizioni Conde Nast S.p.A.*

The hunter's safari jacket was conflated with the American-European explorer's white suit in the tropics. The resulting garment added the jacket's chest and bellows-hip pockets to the original, unembellished suit.

OPPOSITE: Safari jacket and shirt by Angelo Tarlazzi; riding pants by Hackett; leather belt by Mulberry Co.; boots by Hawkins. Fashion editorial published in L'Uomo Vogue, *Milan, February 1988. Photographer: Michael Roberts. Courtesy Edizioni Conde Nast S.p.A.*

RIGHT: Clark Gable in China Seas. *1935. Unknown photographer for MGM. Courtesy Bettmann Archive.*

Self-belted bush pants, part of the hunter's wardrobe, have crossed over into leisure wear and are even adapted as cutoffs for casual use.

ABOVE: Joe Colby in Laurel Canyon. 1987. Photographer: Tom McBride. Courtesy the photographer.

Redford played in *Out of Africa* (1985) could swagger with a kha arrogance. Redford's character was Denys Finch Hatton, the aristocra Englishman who had arrived in Kenya in 1916 and whose love aff with Danish writer Isak Dinesen would be the subject of the film. his role as Finch Hatton, Redford combined rolled-up sleeves, hi boots, broad belts, and shirts with functional pockets, the expedition hunter as a heroic figure: regal, yet ready for action at the same tim

The safari jacket had been codified in the 1920s by the New Yo firm of Willis & Geiger when it created its classic version of the garme modeling it after the British military's field dress. The original sty no. 486, is still in manufacture, and is made of a highly dense cott woven 340 strands to the inch, which gives the cloth water resistan yet still allows it to breathe. The conditions it addresses are Afric heat, cool nights, and the vagaries of weather; furthermore, it provi a degree of protection against animal claws and such dreaded inse as the safari ant. In the mid-1920s, Abercrombie & Fitch Co. a developed a safari jacket, its similarity to the Willis & Geiger mo suggesting that the latter firm was its supplier. The ingenuity of t safari jacket lies not only in its materials but in its minor modificati of the British officer's uniform, including a feature shared by the N folk jacket: the shoulder pleats that allow for arm and shoulder moti while the jacket remains snug and clasped at the waist.

In 1925, big-game hunters such as Mr. and Mrs. Ernest I. King Winona, Minnesota, were undeniably sovereigns of the land as th stood triumphant on the elephant they had "bagged." Women, t wore the bush jacket as they took part in expeditions. In the fi *Mogambo* (1953), the bush jacket became the sign of another sort conquest as Ava Gardner and Grace Kelly, both wearing the dura Willis & Geiger jacket, were attracted to Clark Gable in the role o white hunter. There is a paramilitary aspect to his appearance, featur trousers rolled over low boots and a jacket with a separate belt a commodious pockets at waist and chest. In another venturing gui Gable took the light tropical suit and pith helmet out of the bush a onto the screen in *China Seas* (1935); although the cut of the suit otherwise conventional, its design was modified by the hunter's bell pockets. In the 1970s, adventurers would wear khaki shirts with so of the characteristics of the bush jacket, such as an Yves Saint Laur model (1970) designed for leisure with pockets modified from the sa style.

Khaki has long offered an alternative to denim for casual wear. Kha are the summer dress of the military and the working gear of mer some industries, but they originated in the uniform of the Anglo-Ind army. "Khaki" (the Hindi word for dusty, or dust-colored) calls to m a brown, yellowish-red hue and a somewhat stiff cotton twill. Ch pants, so named for the fabric's supposed origins in China, were pecially popular for casual wear on campuses in the 1950s, and i this softer, lighter-colored version of khaki that is favored in me sportswear today. It is used in bush pants, a style of trousers deri from the safari. Particularly adaptable to tropical regions, they feat a generous cut and a side-fastened self-belt (or one in canvas webbi avoiding the hot and cumbersome leather belt. Bush pants have a resurgence of popularity as shorts in the 1980s, their amplenes cut giving them an easy, full drape. The essence of the safari app ance is the excess of fabric, its voluminous richness serving comfo both extremes of temperature.

The empire of the adventurer has extended across many mark Since 1978, an important source of adventuring clothing has been Banana Republic, a company founded in New York by Mel and Pat Ziegler. Its clothing and marketing are inflected by the romance of hunter's domain and dress. By the mid-1980s, the company was se all the accoutrements of the safari, and for a brief time even offer telephone service reporting the temperature and the health and poli conditions in various parts of the globe. Sales personnel, identifie guides, were expected to meld the shopping trip and its expeditio fantasy. Specific historicism abounds in the company's manufactu for many of its suppliers have made the same items for outfitte sporting expeditions and even for the military. High-fashion ada

If the British hunter Denys Finch Hatton, portrayed in the film *Out of Africa,* could be identified by his safari clothing, so, too, the American hero can be signaled by his Stetson hat. Indiana Jones, at bottom, adds the swagger of this hat to the bravado of the hunter's dress to personify the American swashbuckler.

TOP LEFT: Robert Redford in Out of Africa. *1985. Unknown photographer for Universal Pictures. Courtesy Kobal Collection. BOTTOM LEFT: Harrison Ford in* Raiders of the Lost Ark. *1981. Unknown photographer for Lucasfilm-Paramount Pictures. Courtesy Kobal Collection.*

Perhaps more than any other contemporary author, Ernest Hemingway created characters of great virility as his leading men; his heroes are typically adventurers, solo agents, or enterprising men of the world. Creator, too, of his own image as an adventurer, Hemingway hunted big and small game in Africa and the American West, always dressed for the part.

ABOVE: Ernest Hemingway on a hunting trip. c. 1943. Unknown photographer. Courtesy Bettmann Archive.

The safari jacket enters the realm of high style in late twentieth-century versions that stress the garment's elegance.

RIGHT: Safari jackets, shorts, shirts, and crew-neck by CP Company; boots by Naviglio. Fashion editorial published in L'Uomo Vogue, *Milan, January 1988. Photographer: Aldo Fallai. Courtesy Edizioni Condé Nast S.p.A.* BELOW: *Lord Rufus Isaacs wearing safari jacket and turtleneck by Burberry's. Fashion editorial published in* Vogue Hommes, *Paris, March 1987. Photographer: Lord Snowdon. Courtesy Editions Condé Nast S.A.* OPPOSITE TOP: *Ensemble by Gianfranco Ferre. Fashion editorial published in* L'Uomo Vogue, *Milan, January*

1988. Photographer: Nadir. Courtesy Edizioni Conde Nast S.p.A.

tions of safari styles are also in ample supply, as designers return to the stringent requirements of the traditional jacket with utilitarian and evocative concerns.

Hunters closer to home have seldom held the same allure as those who wear Burmese pith helmets or the outfittings of the African safari, but the more prosaic domestic hunter has endorsed a wide range of garments that have come into popular use, including boots, jackets with ribbed cuffs, visored caps (derived from the more patrician deerstalker), and the Barbour and other water-repellent coats. They have borrowed the lumberjack's plaid flannel shirt, benefiting from its desirable trait of high visibility and its association with the fantastic exploits of Paul Bunyan and other legendary North Woods loggers. In addition, the woodsman's checked shirt has been commandeered as a lining for the water-resistant garment—the plaid lining of the Barbour and the district check of the classic Burberry raincoat, creating a play between the shirt and the shirtlike lining of the outer coat.

As military clothing has been transmogrified into civilian dress, so the clothing of imperial ambitions has passed with surprisingly little political reverberation into the vernacular. The focus has become the specific heroism of the individual rather than the political implications of his act. To show the imperial hunter in the midst of villagers in native dress positions the hunter's attire as a parallel kind of natural clothing, as endemic to the hero's survival as are the natives' robes to theirs.

ABOVE: Man's ensemble, left, by Giorgio Armani; suspender pants by Emporio Armani with Borsalino hat. Fashion editorial published in L'Uomo Vogue, *Milan, March 1982. Photographer: Aldo Fallai. Courtesy Edizioni Conde Nast S.p.A.*

Closer to home, hunters have established a functional wardrobe that is not sportswear but rather clothing accommodated to the particular conditions of hunting and fishing. Frequently sold outside department and clothing stores by mail-order retailers of hunting and fishing gear, such as L. L. Bean, this category of clothing remains closely identified with its original purpose, even though it has been widely adopted for leisure wear.

LEFT: Hunters with bobcats, Beaumont, Texas. c. 1935. Unknown photographer. Courtesy Bettmann Archive. BELOW: Duck hunter, Cape Cod, Massachusetts. c.

1930. Unknown photographer. Court Bettmann Archive.

oduct loyalty, dependability of suppliers, and traditional associa-
s are important matters to the hunter in his choice of clothing. Like
loyalty of the military traditionalist of the British Empire to the
r who has created garments in accordance with military specifica-
s, the hunting wardrobe requires fidelity and allegiance to a sup-
r. L. L. Bean, of Freeport, Maine, is perhaps the best known
erican purveyor of hunting sportswear. Founded in 1912, the com-
y serves its customers primarily through mail order and at such
me that it has its own zip code. The store's tradition of quality is
to a royal warrant. Allegiance to specific style products in hunting
camping is also ardent; the L. L. Bean lace-up boot with leather
and rubber bottom (as well as its offshoot, the low gum shoe) is
spensable to some travelers, whereas other rural adventurers would
be without their "wellies," their knee-high rubber Wellington
s.

The plaid wool shirt, created to
distinguish and thereby protect
hunters in the wilderness, has become a standard item of casual
wear both on campus and outdoors.

*RIGHT: Class outing. 1948. Photogra-
pher: Rita Adrosko. Courtesy Smithsonian Institution. CENTER RIGHT: Hunter
with moose. c. 1947. Unknown photographer. Courtesy Bettmann Archive.
BOTTOM RIGHT: Sterling Hayden. 1949.
Unknown photographer. Courtesy Kobal
Collection.*

The flap-pocketed plaid shirt worn
with chino pants and long-sleeved
undershirt has become so com-
monplace that it must be associated not only with the hunt but
also with the romantic quest.

*ABOVE: Young man and woman. 1984.
Photographer: Marcia Lippman. Courtesy the photographer.*

THE Sports MAN

e role of the sportsman de-
nds from English country life.
depends on an image of the
glish upper classes at leisure,
r clothing suggesting both the
prieties of dress and the free-
n found in experiencing the
asures of nature. By legend,
country gentleman is attired
ch fabrications of wool stuffs,
r colors those of the English
umn. The garment often as-
iated with the Anglo-Ameri-
 aristocracy and the country
 se is the sports jacket, first
 ised in notable distinction
n the business suit, but in
 cleaving to the manner of
 suit with only minor modifi-
ons in fit, detailing, and fab-

t its inception, the sports
ket was part of the hunting at-
 of a nineteenth-century
ke of Norfolk. In the 1880s,
Norfolk suit, including jack-
knickers, and matching cap,
 worn by the English gentry
n shooting game. In every
se a suit, the outfit met the
cific demands of the hunt,
ing robust materials, often in
 rful plaids and patterns, and
 of fit, facilitating the tramp

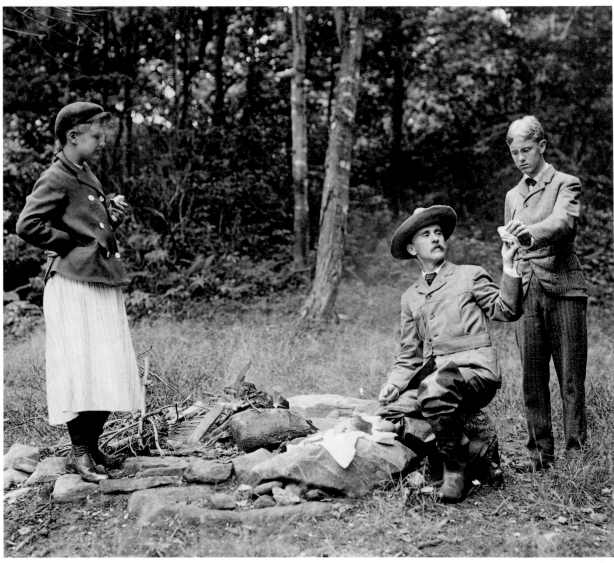

ugh the fields. The jacket of the Norfolk suit was specifically de-
ed for shooting; a sack coat with box pleats front and back, brought
 ther at the waist by a self-belt, it provided for the full mobility of
 hunter's arms as he took aim with the gun. Made of heavy wool, it
 worn without an outer coat in the English autumn. Its tones were
 se of the woods and fields, in clear differentiation from the colors
 n in business. Brown, eschewed in urban dress for men, was the
 eminent color of the sportsman, with possible variations in ginger,
 stard, and heather hues, otherwise taboo in the male wardrobe.
 y the early years of the twentieth century, the gentry's acclamation
 he Norfolk style was directed to the jacket, most often worn with
 natched pants of a sporting style. The romance of the outdoors,
 etimes more civilized than one would have imagined, gave the
 folk jacket a special elan associated with the adventuresome and
 casual. But it was also a most redolently hierarchical garment. It is
 naps no accident that the preferred costume of Norfolk, the premier

The Norfolk jacket, derived from
the rural hunting suit of a nineteenth-century Duke of Norfolk,
has become a widely interpreted
staple of men's sportswear.

*OPPOSITE: Advertisement for Antonio
Miro. 1988. Photographer: Antoni Bernad. Courtesy Antonio Miro. TOP: The
Douglas Fairbanks, Senior and Junior.
c. 1929. Unknown photographer. Courtesy Kobal Collection. CENTER: Henry
van Dyke and young campers. 1903.
Photographer: T. E. Mort. Courtesy Library of Congress. BOTTOM: F. Scott
Fitzgerald. 1925. Unknown photographer. Published in Vanity Fair, July
1925. Courtesy Condé Nast Publications,
Inc.*

Basketweave, above, and glen plaid, opposite, represent two textile possibilities for men's sports jackets, the aggressive patterns reinforcing the wearer's break with traditional business dress.

ABOVE: Gary Cooper. 1937. Photographer: William Walling, Jr., for Paramount Pictures. Courtesy Kobal Collection.

dukedom of England, ranking next after the princes of royal bloo would have been widely adopted by the gentry. The man who wear Norfolk jacket partakes of a certain tradition, in the same way that t man who wears a Harris tweed (and who would, of course, wear no ot er) not only dwells in the Highlands but specifically in the Outer H brides, where the handweaving tradition goes back one hundred ar fifty years.

As the 1920s progressed, the Norfolk style was adopted for skiing the American actor and noted Anglophile Douglas Fairbanks, Jr., wl was photographed on the ski slopes with his equally famous father. T Norfolk was seized on by young men immediately out of college, pe haps in emulation of such figures as F. Scott Fitzgerald, wearing t jacket in a photograph taken by *Vanity Fair* in 1925; the twenty-nin year-old writer exudes the self-confidence of the young and fit (and the newly published: his *Great Gatsby* had just appeared), even as wears the tie and white shirt we associate with business dress. Fitzgera stuffs his hands into his side pockets in a casual gesture unlikely ir business suit; deep patch pockets accommodate hands and gloves, well as business notes.

As the social hunt became more compelling for the twentieth centu than the pursuit of game, the Norfolk became domesticated. The spo jacket emerged, maintaining a distinctiveness in fabrication anc slightly boxy fit but nonetheless abandoning the Norfolk's box ple: in favor of the more conventional lines of the sack suit. The should were fuller, sleeves wider, and armholes larger, but this jacket pledg allegiance to the suit style—and became a state of mind as much a matter of recreation. It gave color and pattern to men's clothing a provided an opportunity to dress for an occasion other than busine The keen desire to maintain the separation between the sports jac and the daily dress of business still obtains within many professio When the advertising and other creative professions allowed a fi stage informality to invade office wear during the 1960s, the spo jacket achieved some recognition as business clothing. But with many professions have resisted its possible incursion, insisting that place is with country weekends and recreations. And the Establishme is correct in eschewing the sports jacket: its intention is subversive is ultimately about style and leisure rather than sports. Gatsby's g appellation of "sport" for his men friends was to identify them as tea mates and companions—sporting men, perhaps, but sportsman? N

Beyond silhouette, the sports jacket is an important expression freedom within the sphere of men's clothing. It offers an opportur for personal expression, at times even to the point of caricature. Eve one knows a man who dresses impeccably when given the constrain choices of business attire but goes wild with flashy, boldly pattern or otherwise outrageous choices in his leisure wear. Individual st prevails in casual dress in a manner disallowed in business. Its expr sion may be as simple as the wearing of a dress shirt and tie with a tw jacket, but it extends to other possibilities, such as adding sweater create layered dress or experimenting with an ascot or related strateg of the scarf, sleeve and shoulder patches, and other surface decoration

Movie stars of the 1930s and 1940s wore sports jackets that defin their individual styles. Gary Cooper may be seen in the fey gestur wearing a tie belt with a loud plaid jacket, and in an even more imm erate manner, adding an alluring ascot to his sporting costume in a ductive scene with Tallulah Bankhead—who wears evening cloth Robert Taylor's dashing nonchalance in draping a rayon scarf arou his neck and turning up the collar of his jacket is an insouciant gestu succeeding because it was so unconventional at the time. Sper Tracy, however, reveals a mismatched discomfort in displaying an necessary pocket handkerchief and letting his collar flap over and un his jacket lapels on either side; indeed, he wears a jacket insuffici to make its own style statement—although generations of won would assert that Tracy's style required little assistance from his cloth Nevertheless, many man agree that the greater a jacket's styling, greater is its distinction. Indeed, men of style have allowed the sp jacket to speak loudly their style message. The comfortable nonc lance of Frank Sinatra and Montgomery Clift relaxing in their cas

...eeds is the essence of style, reflecting self-confidence and independence.

As English country life and the sport of shooting had provided the ...gins of the sports jacket, so it also governed the fabrics used, includ-... robust tweeds, shepherd's checks, and houndstooth, all offering ...ages of the country even in their names. Eventually, cotton jackets ...re introduced for summer, but the bright solids, madras plaids, and ...rsucker textures chosen lack the country-house insinuation of the ...avy jackets.

The unmatched jacket for all seasons is the blue blazer. Its classic ...tus is confirmed in the wardrobe advice given successive generations ...young men entering the social and business worlds: they will find the ...zer an indispensable link between the two worlds, for under extreme ...cumstances it can pass for business dress when mixed, in a stretch of ...vention, with a pair of gray slacks. Nevertheless, the blazer is de-...ed from the outdoors and leisure's styles. The sporting garment of ...formity, it owes its genesis, according to legend, to the British Navy. ...the nineteenth century, the captain of the HMS *Blazer*, anticipating ...isit by Queen Victoria, found his crew a motley throng and dressed ...em in like blue-serge jackets. The legend asserts that these blue ...kets were named blazers after the frigate and after their marked suc-...s as naval dress. Although the story is unlikely, the legend condenses ...ore epic history that may have migrated from the seas but also from ...playing fields and reefer jackets of preparatory schools and colleges, ...h minor mutations entering the picture from military uniforms. The ...zer lends itself to a heraldic identification through pocket emblems, ...more democratic blazers enjoy modernist anonymity. Brass buttons ...y represent a family, a club, or a branch of the military (in a vestige ...the blazer as a military expression). Unlike the sports jacket, the ...zer expresses uniformity; it also suggests the company and congeries ...men, but men in their valiant identity with the sea or the team. When ...rn with white pants, the blazer betokens the sea. Relaxed movie ...rs, socialites, and athletes have favored white trousers—flannel for ...ter and white duck for summer—with a savoir faire now only par-...ly mitigated by the wearing of this costume by countless glee clubs ...d high-school graduates. The white flannels also made an immediate ...nsition to sports such as tennis and provided a flexible pair of odd ...users that could be used in a variety of situations. The blue blazer ...traditionally been available in single- and double-breasted styles, ...latter perhaps even jauntier than the former. Generations of spiffy ...n have worn the blazer as a classic with versatility and a strong sense ...radition.

...Varm weather has offered certain other sporting alternatives to men, ...luding the seersucker suit. Transplanted from the tropics to summer ...ar in Newport and winter in Palm Beach, the familiar blue-and-white ...ton suit has long been associated with languorous Southern gran-...s, elegant despite sweltering weather. According to fashion writer ...Bruce Boyer, writing in 1985, "the only thing that's changed about ...seersucker suit over the past fifty years has been the price." Yet its ...ular appeal has always been suspect. Damon Runyon, who favored ...style in the 1940s, claimed that it reconciled the very rich and the ...y poor, but was seldom worn by those in between. He found that the ...ate wrinkle of the rumpled cotton suggested either a terrible want ...grand will.

...he origin of the name is Persian (*shir-o-shakkar*, literally milk and ...ar, or smooth and sweet in alternation, like the texture). The soft ...tructured fabric has been worn in the business offices of warm cli-...es for many years, although the now all-pervasive presence of air ...ditioning has no doubt reduced the need for lighter fabrics. The suit ...y still bear the imprimatur of Princeton (the favored Ivy League ...ool of Southern aristocrats) and the natural hegemony of cotton, but ...ariations in synthetic fabrics almost overwhelmed its reputation in ...late 1950s. Discerning consumers understood quickly, however, ...difference between the flat, uncreasing synthetics and their soft ...rsucker source.

...ess discerning, however, are the wearers of other styles appropri-...d from upper-class recreations and brought into wide acceptance in

ABOVE: *Gary Cooper and Tallulah Bankhead in* Devil and the Deep. *1932. Unknown photographer for Paramount Pictures. Courtesy Kobal Collection.*

Continued on page 121

As Spencer Tracy demonstrates, the tweed jacket is the all-purpose foil for odd trousers. Tracy's influence on clothing from the early 1930s onward emanated from his movie roles as a congenial man of the people, a creature of tweeds and other casual attire at business and leisure. In its fascination with texture and the informality of the ensemble, a 1930s portrait of screen actor Robert Taylor could almost pass for 1980s fashion advertising. The insouciant mingling of wool windowpane jacket, silk pocket square, rayon scarf, and knit sweater worn next to the skin creates a complexity of grain and sportswear motifs. The assertive herringbone pattern of Frank Sinatra's sports jacket contributes to its tough message. The vestigial top button, atrophied in most modern sports jackets, allows Sinatra to be buttoned cockily at the collar.

TOP: *Spencer Tracy. 1934. Photographer: Imogen Cunningham. Published in* Vanity Fair, *December 1934. © 1934 (renewed 1962) Condé Nast Publications, Inc.* ABOVE: *Robert Taylor. c. 1935. Photographer: Ted Allan. Courtesy Staley-Wise Gallery.* RIGHT: *Frank Sinatra. 1944. Photograher: Philippe Halsman. © 1989 Yvonne Halsman.*

Montgomery Clift, at left, is a figure almost impossible to situate in time, so universal is the stylishly casual standard of his button-down shirt, loosened tie, and patterned sports jacket. At top and right, the sports jacket in a double-breasted style is paired with white flannels to achieve a sporting appearance for Corey Ford and Clark Gable.

TOP: Writer Corey Ford. 1930. Unknown photographer. Courtesy Library of Congress. ABOVE: Clark Gable. 1931. Photographer: George Hurrell for MGM. Courtesy Kobal Collection and Staley-Wise Gallery. LEFT: Montgomery Clift. 1950. Photographer: Hymie Fink. Courtesy Staley-Wise Gallery.

The perfect all-purpose garment because it can be worn for dress or on informal occasions, the blue blazer in its single- and double-breasted forms suggests both the aristocratic world of private yacht-ing and the more democratic sphere of naval service.

TOP LEFT: *Singer Bing Crosby. c. 1935. Unknown photographer for Paramount Pictures. Courtesy Kobal Collection.* BOTTOM LEFT: *Radio crooner Will Os-born. c. 1925. Photographer: Underwood and Underwood. Courtesy Library of Congress.* BELOW: *Men in blue blazers and white flannels. Fashion editorial p... lished in* GQ, *New York, April 198... Photographer: Pamela Hanson. Cour... Condé Nast Publications, Inc.*

en at a hot-weather resort, erican aristocrat Anthony J. exel Biddle, Jr., above, stead-ly maintained such protocols of ss as tie, collar pin, and rolled, ressed cuffs, but he and many is compatriots sensibly adopted arm-weather fabric called seer-ker for their suits. Palm Beach, Florida resort redolent of new nk and social status, became a loquial reference and eventually rand name for summer clothing. e quiet reserve of men's dress is ersed when it comes to sports thing: Nantucket red or lime-en pants, madras and pieced-dras jackets and trousers, fauna-ked trousers in bright colors, unexpected shorts shout their ependence from accustomed d taste. Social historian Paul ssell describes this characteristic eing a sign of the eminent aris-racy of the upper class and its ity to be boorish and get away h it.

VE: Anthony J. Drexel Biddle, Jr., his wife, Mary Duke Biddle. c. 1925. nown photographer. Courtesy Bett-n Archive. CENTER RIGHT: Tail-s Jamie Jeremiah, Neal Carney, and Hogan in madras at the Foxfield Course, Charlottesville, Virginia. ished in M, New York, July 1985. ographer: George Chinsee. Courtesy rchild Syndication. TOP RIGHT: modore Robert Stone of the New York t Club in Nantucket reds and boat

shoes. Published in M, New York, Jan-uary 1985. Unknown photographer. Courtesy Fairchild Syndication. BOTTOM RIGHT: Man in red Bermuda shorts and crested navy blazer. Published in M, New York, September 1986. Photographer: George Chinsee. Courtesy Fairchild Syn-dication.

postwar period. With the headline "Evolution hits a cul de sac [in] ~~hly~~ specialized drone WASPS in Newport, R.I.," the men's fashion ~~magazine~~ *M* took note of the wearing of outlandishly decorated trousers ~~with~~ blazers and Top-Siders, an old style that was seemingly never ~~ending~~. Nantucket Reds, the red-cotton trousers that may once have ~~had~~ sporting swagger, had become beacons of bad taste. But Top-Sid- ~~ers~~, the deck shoes invented in 1939 by yachtsman Paul Sperry, remain ~~forever~~ new; created to provide steady traction on board ship by means of ~~her~~ringbone-shaped channels in the sole, the durable shoes have been ~~worn~~ by sailing enthusiasts (such as John F. Kennedy) ever since. De- ~~cora~~tive in their innocent, workmanlike configuration, these service- ~~abl~~e shoes have sailed from the yachting upper crust to campus and ur- ~~ban~~ life.

~~B~~eyond the sea (and yet not too far), the East Coast Establishment ~~has~~ established a beachhead on Bermuda. Bermuda shorts are a modern ~~alte~~rnative to slacks, a compromise between athletic shorts and long ~~trou~~sers. The extreme version of Bermuda shorts as a trousers substitute ~~is t~~he semipatrician style of combining them with jacket and tie—in the ~~193~~0s they were worn (accompanied by knee-high socks) with dinner ~~jac~~kets. Bermuda being British in its associations, the proprieties of is- ~~lan~~d law required that the shorts begin no more than two inches above ~~the~~ knee, assuring them to be scrupled, regulated attire—not frivolous ~~or s~~alacious. At a considerably farther reach, the Mediterranean also ~~enr~~iched the wardrobe of the sportsman of style, as even the Duke of ~~Wi~~ndsor took on yachting stripes, bringing them ashore in Portofino. ~~Ev~~en if the garment, a blue-and-white striped jersey, originated with ~~a~~ crew (and especially the romantic gondoliers of Venice), its early ~~app~~ropriation by the rakish, even stylish Picasso and his elegant Anglo-~~Sax~~on friend, Gerald Murphy, gave it a cachet that ever separated it ~~fro~~m the proletarian undershirt, whence it came.

~~T~~he idle rich have always been preoccupied with sports and the pro- ~~ge~~nitors of style. Even when their sporting habits could not be imitated, ~~the~~ir sporting habiliments could be. No single sport better indicates this ~~tran~~sformation of leisure into style than tennis. The noted tennis writer ~~Wa~~yne Kalyn refers to the "champagne-and-caviar game of tennis" to ~~des~~cribe the origins of the game and the nature of its dress until the ~~193~~0s. Originally, men wore neckties on the tennis court, as well as stiff-~~coll~~ar shirts; long trousers were favored until several years into the ~~192~~0s, with white flannels the required pants for the sport. The shirt ~~that~~ transformed tennis dress was designed in 1926 by the twenty-one-~~yea~~r-old international champion (and inveterate inventor) René La-~~cos~~te. Even though the young Frenchman retired from the game in ~~192~~9, his nickname and shirt have become classics of the sport. Lacoste ~~was~~ called *le Crocodile* for his tennis acumen and aggressiveness; he ~~em~~blazoned his shirts and even his white jacket with a symbol of the ~~nic~~kname he had been given. In 1933, the shirt entered the market-~~plac~~e and met a need not only for the game of tennis but for a cool, re-~~silie~~nt shirt in cotton that would allow the wearer to be active and yet ~~com~~fortable. One feature of Lacoste's first shirt has prevailed in the ~~suc~~ceeding production: a long tail assures that the shirt stays tucked in ~~at t~~he back even with a strenuous stroke. In a 1970s style reversal, a ~~non~~chalant preppy look favored wearing the Lacoste shirt with tail ex-~~pos~~ed, and the asymmetry of front and back became a nonfunctional ~~pos~~e as much as a tennis necessity. The original Lacoste shirt respected ~~ten~~nis white, though its derivations have exploited the worn and faded ~~colo~~rs of cotton piqué. As the Lacoste shirt has expanded beyond its ~~sp~~ort of origin, its name has become a generic term to describe any ver-~~sati~~le cotton tennis shirt (almost invariably with emblem) with a two-~~or t~~hree-button placket and ribbed collar.

~~B~~y the 1970s, the Lacoste shirt had become a cliché of preppy style ~~rem~~oved from tennis-court snobbery. Indeed, tennis itself had been ~~dem~~ocratized by the increase in public tennis courts and rising affluence ~~of t~~he postwar period. So stuck was the bond between class and croc-~~odil~~e that an antipreppy design sported a canceled alligator. Thus, the ~~shir~~t that challenged convention in the late 1920s (albeit emanating ~~from~~ the upper class) had become the convention to be challenged in ~~the~~ 1970s. Nonetheless, the tennis shirt remains a staple of men's

In the 1920s, the sailor's striped T-shirt was lifted from its proletarian origins by the international set in residence along the Mediterranean. With its idiosyncratically wide, high-cut neckline (called the bateau), elbow-length or slightly longer sleeves, and horizontal, blue-and-white stripes, the style has long been a staple of men's sportswear, and is equally popular in its crossover to women's wear. Perhaps owing to its slightly rakish European origins, this style is closely associated with artists.

TOP: *The Duke of Windsor in Portofino. 1951. Photographer: Thurston Hopkins. Courtesy Bettmann Archive.* CENTER: *Pablo Picasso. c. 1948. Photographer: Robert Capa. Courtesy Magnum Photos, Inc.* RIGHT: *Andy Warhol outside the Factory. 1968. Photographer: Bob Adelman. Courtesy Magnum Photos, Inc.*

The "New Wasp" wears the full regalia of upper-class leisure while leaning on a George I chair in Mrs. Winston Frederick Churchill Guest's topiary garden at Templeton. Not-too-neat by intent, this country gentleman is a sloppy aristocrat at play in clothing worn with uncaring aplomb.

OPPOSITE: *The "New Wasp." Jacket by Paul Stuart; shorts by Ralph Lauren; shirt by Perry Ellis Men; sweater by Bill Robinson. Fashion editorial published in* Vanity Fair, *New York, May 1986. Photographer: Arthur Elgort. © 1986 Arthur Elgort.*

For decades, tennis remained an upper-crust sport, its gentility expressed through the elegant white clothing familiarly called "tennis whites." Since the 1960s, white shirts and white-flannel trousers have given way to more individua and even multicolored apparel.

Dubbed *Le Crocodile* by the sports press as early as 1923 after making a bet involving an alligator-hide suitcase, French tennis champion René Lacoste earned the nickname by his tenacity on the court His friend Robert George drew an alligator that was embroidered fir on Lacoste's blazer and subsequently, in 1926, on the white piqué-jersey tennis shirt Lacoste invented for his own use. The original design featured the ribbe collar, short sleeves with ribbed bands, and alligator emblem still found on the Lacoste shirt today. Popular in France from its commercial introduction in 1933, the shirt was first marketed in the United States in 1952 and later manufactured in America under license beginning in 1966. More than 200 million Lacoste shirts have been sold worldwide, with control and management of the firm still in the hands of the Lacoste family.

LEFT: *French lawn-tennis player R Lacoste and Takeichi Harada of Japan the West Side Tennis Club in Forest H. New York, after their Davis Cup matc which Lacoste was defeated. 1926. known photographer. Courtesy Bettma Archive.*

wardrobes (and is worn by women as well). The versatility of the tennis shirt is also revealed in its alternate name, the polo shirt.

Similarly, the cable-knit tennis sweater is also known as a cricket sweater and is, in fact, the uniform of cricket. One sport yielded its apparel to another, and the identity of a tennis team could as easily be determined by its sweaters as could a cricket team by theirs. The cream or white cable-knit sweater with bands at the collar and waist in blue and maroon was more than simple sports apparel—it had the comfortable sense of being the clothing to wear before or after the match. In the 1920s and 1930s, the American tennis champion Bill Tilden popularized the tennis sweater and ratified its affiliation with tennis above all other sports. At more or less the same time the Prince of Wales had taken to wearing the tennis sweater for sundry informal occasions and provided the opportunity for it to move away from sports entirely, again trailing its upper-class associations and its V-neck pullover comfort. The movie star Robert Stack, in the 1950s, was able to express the sunny and sporting pleasures of Southern California in wearing the tennis sweater, even if he did not belong to any traditional club. And in the 1980s, designer Bill Blass suggested suburban and sophisticated elegance in his combination of jeans, tennis sweater, dog, and mission furniture, a compelling mix of leisure's signs, all with the supreme sanction of upper-class respectability. Although there is no perfect formula for the tennis sweater, its classic status was confirmed in the 1970s and 1980s after a brief flamboyant interval when, under the influence of the 1960s Peacock Revolution, it underwent peach, sunny-yellow, and baby-blue permutations. That none of these obtained affirms the viability of the traditional style. Its survival in the 1980s was of nuanced fashionability, but the fundamental garment had remained intact for nearly a century.

Golf, with links to wealth, heritage, and clubs, has served as a fertile ground for sportsmen's styles. The tennis sweater was austere in its regimen compared to the favored golf sweater. In the 1920s, the Prince of Wales brought popularity to the Fair Isle sweater by wearing it for golf. The knitting industry of the small island, located to the north of the Scottish mainland, between the Shetland and the Orkney islands, was perhaps saved by the Prince's gesture. The Fair Isle patterns were widely supposed to have originated with Spanish sailors stranded by the defeat of the Armada in 1588, but there is seemingly no substance to this knit epic. Rather, the making of the myth may have occurred in the mid-nineteenth century, when a vocabulary of patterning based, it would seem, on some local inventions carefully transcribed in pattern books, once more became popular. Employing rows of abstract, geometric patterns, the first examples described date from the 1850s and 1860s, but the earliest examples of Fair Isle knits to survive are socks, caps, and cuffs of roughly 1870. The Prince of Wales was frequently photographed in his favorite Fair Isle V-neck pullovers, but contemporary versions also included cardigans and crewnecks, as well as a range of hose and accessories.

Golf was never able to transfer knickers to town. Although they were worn on golf courses in the 1920s (and in rare instances are today), they were not generated by that sport; rather, they were a modification of hunting garb. Manicured greens and carefully trimmed fairways do not warrant the wearing of trousers invented for rougher sport. But although knickers were deemed superfluous for golf, they were adopted for a time by children and dandies, both tremulous associations for modern men. The brief popularity of knickers faded away when champion golfers such as Bobby Jones favored long trousers. In recurrent revival, the knickers style is rarely associated with the game that adopted it so briefly.

There has always been a romance and a metaphor attached to the hunt. In the early years of the century, walking and hunting suits worn in the English countryside took on the burly and gruff fabrics of the fall season. Sports jackets were amply proportioned for layered dressing and for ease in shooting. Knickers accommodated high socks and boots. Although ever debonair (and never failing to maintain coat and tie), the hunter was outfitted with necessity in mind: the impediments of weather, mud, and portage were all accommodated by his clothing. Tweeds and earth colors served as natural camouflage. As the style was revived in the 1980s, it maintained the aura of gentility. The fabrics available to the sportsman were many. Knits, especially adaptable to changes in the weather, were available in handmade, corrugated textures suggestive of the ridging and grooves of natural forms. Even for the city, the materials of the countryside dictated the gentleman's attire. Stout fabrics such as corduroy with wide ribs suggested the brawny stuff of the outdoors; bold tweeds referred to the surfaces of nature; leather buttons and patches returned the gentleman to the skins of conquest; and bold plaids even invoked the majesty and notorious gallantry and savagery of the Highland warrior.

Much of the clothing worn by modern man come from the fields of hunt and play. The attire mandated by these activities has often merged with fanciful notions of country style, transforming sports attire into clothing suitable to be worn under any circumstance. Even as its sporting roots may atrophy, clothing that once outfitted the sportsman now adjusts to manifold service in the male wardrobe.

The classic V-neck tennis sweater, s neckline underscored by blue-nd-red striping, first became pop-lar on and off the court in the 920s. Appropriated from the sport f cricket, the sweater's form has emained basically unchanged nce its introduction nearly a cen-ry ago.

In a rare instance of an entire industry having been revived by one man's wardrobe, the Fair Isle sweater was made popular in the 1920s when the Prince of Wales took up the style for wear with tweeds for golf. An adventurous dresser, the Prince combined the patterned sweater with plaid or tweed knickers and highly colored hose. Social critic Alison Lurie once described golf as the sport of the flagrantly wealthy; it removes lands from cultivation, manicures nature to aesthetic excess, and requires of the player expensive equipment.

ABOVE: The Prince of Wales with, left right, General Trotter, Lord Sinclair, a Brig. Gen. Sir Robert Gordon Gilmour Muirfield golf course in East Lothi Scotland. c. 1925. Unknown photog pher. Courtesy Bettmann Archive. LE Edward, Prince of Wales. c. 1925. U known photographer. Courtesy Library Congress.

ickers, earlier a general resort
sporting style, became identi-
with golf in the 1920s, but
re soon supplanted by less ex-
me trousers. As golf, like tennis,
came popular, it "escaped" from
vate clubs to municipal courses,
with the advent of television,
ame a widely followed specta-
sport. Professional golf cham-
ns such as Bobby Jones and Ar-
d Palmer replaced blue bloods
tyle setters. Palmer's cardigan
ater became so well recognized
emulated that he decided to
duce his own line of sportswear.

*: Frank White, Treasurer of the
ted States, golfing. c. 1926. Unknown
tographer. Courtesy Library of Con-
s. RIGHT: Champion golfer Arnold
mer. Published in Sports Illustrated,
York, September 1, 1969. Photog-
er: Gerry Cranham. Courtesy Time
BOTTOM: Champion golfer Robert
bby) Tyre Jones, Jr. c. 1930. Photog-
er: Nickolas Muray. Courtesy Inter-
ional Museum of Photography at
ge Eastman House.*

The hunt in all its forms is the stylized sport of conquest and survival. The etiquette and polite savagery of shooting, like the clothing the sport engenders, are overlaid with an aura of aristocratic tradition. But the extreme refinements of the garments are determined by the physical demands of movement, terrain, and climate.

TOP: Edward, Prince of Wales. c. 1920. Unknown photographer. Courtesy Bettmann Archive. CENTER: Mr. Bradley Martin at a shooting party at Coombe Abbey, the estate of the Earl and Countess of Craven, in England. c. 1920. Unknown photographer. Courtesy Bettmann Archive. RIGHT: Mr. G. Livingston with his bird dog. c. 1920. Unknown photographer. Courtesy Smithsonian Institution.

Ernest Hemingway wears a modified Norfolk jacket in herringbone tweed with expandable back pleats, suede sleeves with knit cuffs, and patch pockets protectively trimmed with suede.

ABOVE: Ernest Hemingway with his labrador. c. 1930. Photographer: Robert Capa. Courtesy Magnum Photos, Inc.

The glamour of the pursuit, rustic yet refined, is echoed in the beauty of the walking suit. Functional yet self-consciously quaint, the country walking suit carries with it a nostalgia for a life of Arcadian perfection and can be seen as the clothing equivalent of the picturesque.

ABOVE: Ensemble by Confitri. Fashion editorial published in Uomo Harper's Bazaar, *Milan, July–August 1985. Photographer: Bob Krieger. Courtesy Edizioni Syds-Italia s.r.l. TOP RIGHT: Country-look ensembles by Ralph Lauren. Fashion editorial published in* GQ, *New York, September 1981. Photographer: Barry McKinley. Courtesy Condé Nast Publications, Inc. BOTTOM RIGHT: English country scene. c. 1980. Photographer: David Hurn. Courtesy Magnum Photos, Inc. OPPOSITE: Ensemble by Niko. Fashion editorial published in* Uomo Harper's Bazaar, *Milan, January–February 1987. Photographer: Peter Zander. Courtesy Edizioni Syds-Italia s.r.l.*

Garments suitable for urban life may be rendered for the country gentleman in harder, more durable materials appropriate to withstanding the elements in the countryside.

OPPOSITE: Edward, Prince of Wales. c. 1920. Unknown photographer. Courtesy Bettmann Archive. ABOVE LEFT: Advertisement for Corneliani. 1982. Photographer: Aldo Fallai. Courtesy Corneliani. ABOVE RIGHT: Ensemble by Enrico Coveri. Published in Uomo Harper's Bazaar, *Milan, July–August 1987. Photographer: Peter Zander. Courtesy Edizioni Syds-Italia s.r.l.*

The pieces that comprise the country gentleman's wardrobe evoke tradition, but favorites may be interchanged and recombined in new and personal ways.

CENTER: Italian country sportswear [...] fashion editorial published in L'U[...] Vogue, Milan, November 1980. [...] tographer: Aldo Fallai. Courtesy [...] zioni Condé Nast S.p.A. TOP LEFT[...] rolean sweater by Hobo; hooded coe[...] Berg; polo shirt by Ates Tricots. [...] RIGHT: Jacket by Quantas; sweate[...] Fusione; scarf by Prochownick; glo[...] Portolano. LEFT: Hunting jacke[...] Maremma; leather pants by Cor[...] sweater by Fusione. OPPOSITE: D[...] Chatto wearing ensemble by Had[...] Fashion editorial published in Vc[...] Hommes, Paris, March 1987. Ph[...] rapher: Lord Snowdon. Courtesy [...] Editions Condé Nast S.A.

JOE COLLEGE

The best years of our lives, by aphorism at least, are those just preceding adulthood. For the male, who in the waning decades of the twentieth century is apt to be college-educated, the college years may serve as the last youthful idyll. The clothing associated with this latently adult, potentially omnipotent, and yet wondrously free young man has made its mark on men's fashion. Joe College—an expression that probably originated in songs of the "Roaring Twenties"—conjures up different pictures: fraternal relaxation, rough-and-tumble sports, and formal outings and proms. Sports inevitably enter into the collegiate ideal, even if one is only the spectator, and a kind of infectious idealism known as "school spirit" inspires camaraderie with the team, the class, and the school. Team fellowship also evokes nostalgic imagery, if only as a lament for and recollection of youth. Sports insignia are specifically associated with Joe College, the cherished letter sweater not only representing achievement in sports, but also asserting territoriality in love and membership in an elite group—identified by a single letter.

The raccoon coat is the only fur coat ascribed fully to the modern male. Collegiate men wore fur coats in the second decade of this century in an anachronistic suggestion of the idyll of the New England college in winter, and the coat has flourished as a sign of the 1920s. In that decade, as the college-educated in America expanded in number, the raccoon coat was the rakish dress of the collegiate male for the all-important sports events of fall and winter. The cartoons of illustrator John Held, Jr., published in *The New Yorker*, *The New York Times*, and many other well-known periodicals, made the raccoon coat as much a sign of the Jazz Age as bobbed hair on women. By the 1980s, men would again elect to wear the fur coat, sanctioned not by dandy extravagance wherein the coat has always had some limited viability, but by its associations with youth. In a contemporary photograph by Marcia Lippman, the same dapper spirit popularized by John Held inspires a collegian wearing a letter sweater, porkpie hat, bow tie, and raccoon coat; it is as if he had been seated in the bleachers for nearly seventy-five years. This wraith of the unquenchable college spirit is ever young and ever present in the male imagination.

Loafers, pipes, chino pants, and sweaters worn with tweed jackets are the standard for male dress on campus. If the styles of the sweaters vary, if one generation permits torn blue jeans whereas another, in a collegiate lifetime some four years before, had allowed only pressed chinos, it is clear that the casual nature of collegiate dress is based on two codes, the measurement by peers and the simulation of adult styles. Thus, if the raccoon coat seemed festive in the 1920s, it was because it was a remembrance of a male style of some three decades before, when the most prosperous men wore furs. If in the 1940s undergraduate sweaters at Syracuse University, in New York, wore the same styles as those advocated by the Prince of Wales in the 1930s, all the better.

Man and boy in the same instant and same outfit, Joe College wears such classic styles as the penny loafer, which has remained unchanged for more than half a century. Social critic John Sedgwick rightly acknowledges: "Fashion has no place in the Ivy League wardrobe." If there is an option, it is between the classic and absurd, never an evo-

THE SATURDAY EVENING POST

An Illustrated Weekly Magazine
Founded A.º D.ᴵ 1728 ... Franklin

JUNE 29, 1907   5c. THE COPY

From the turn of the century, the Big Man on Campus laid claim to achievement writ large in the letter sweater. The letter denoted initiation and acceptance as well as individual accomplishment in a sport. Although the letter sweater was sometimes a turtleneck in a "beefy" sweater material (thus adding to the brawn of the athlete), its definitive form was the cardigan, often given to the girl of the athlete's choice in dating rituals. One of the major characteristics of Joe College's dress in the years before the Second World War, the letter sweater had social cachet until it was "debased" by its similar appropriation in high schools.

lution such as fashion. The Ivy Leaguer, says Sedgwick, "is really buying an ethic" in his clothing choices. The ethic is a Puritanical anti-fashion conviction that classic garments should continue in the contemporary wardrobe like a college's well-established and unquestioned curriculum.

Like goldfish swallowing and phone-booth stuffing, men's fashions of the college years tend to be faddish. Madras jackets or shorts, narrow bow ties, flapping shirttails, sockless shoes and sneakers, wide-legged Oxford trousers, Bermuda shorts, and cutoff jeans are among the countless fads for men that have originated on college campuses, where the intellectual and social experiment inevitably includes men's unconstrained imaginations about clothing. Joe College can be peculiar, far out, or radical according to his own choosing.

However outrageous he may be, Joe College also has the future on his mind. He need not be Alex Keaton, a rapacious character from the television series "Family Ties" (1983-89), to realize that the world be-

Ribbed
Interwoven Socks

COPYRIGHT BY INTERWOVEN STOCKING COMPANY

yond college holds standards and expectations in clothing as in all else. In 1940, actor James Stewart donned the garb of Joe College—a yellow sweater vest, blue shirt, black tie, black-and-white pin-checked jacket, and pleated, white-flannel pants—but this carefully orchestrated youthful ensemble held the promise of both extremes, either the tasteful man in the gray-flannel suit or the more flamboyant dandy, so precocious was Stewart in his acceptance of the nuanced dressing of the adult male. More than a quarter of a century later, actor Dustin Hoffman, as Benjamin in *The Graduate* (1967), returned home from campus in a poly-blend seersucker suit, black-knit tie, and blue button-down shirt, a collegian who seemed to harken to both the siren of "plastic" and the vamping of a friend's mother. Collegians like to leave their options open: the repp ties and chinos may be preserved for a way of life, liberated from trunks for suitable reunions, or packed away forever with the things of childhood as fond memories of days past. Through the 1960s, men's fashion magazines offered formulaic components for college apparel. In 1962, *Esquire* insisted that a basic college wardrobe included one dark-blue suit (preferably with vest); a medium gray flannel; a patterned suit; a navy blazer; a checked, plaid, or striped-Shetland or tweed jacket; and numerous other matters, including fifteen shirts ("6 white button-down Oxford cloth, 3 blue, 1 yellow or olive, and 3 striped; 2 tab collars in white, or white with stripes, broadcloth") and such indispensables of college life as formal wear (including patent pumps) for evening and twenty pairs of socks. In September 1968, the year of world-wide student dissent against the war in Vietnam, the same journal would retaliate against student discontent at Columbia University in a feature headed: "Students for a Stylish Society" which commenced: "Not every undergraduate at Morningside Heights [Columbia University] is an affront to the eye, a stench in the nostrils." Clearly, there are those who would come dressed as Ivy Leaguers to any social revolution, content in the impeccable blue blazer, gray flannels, and Bass Weejuns with or without athletic socks.

The impact of Joe College extends far beyond the specific interval of the college years. Long after being a Harvard undergraduate, Senator John Kennedy continued to express the youthful collegiate style that for men of the American upper class and upper-middle class began even before college in preparatory school, whence the notion of the "preppy" look. Barefoot and wearing chino shorts and an open-collared button-down shirt, Kennedy brought the campus spirit and the engaging vitality of youth to the adult forum of national politics. Today's rolled chinos and blue jeans with the cuffs turned up still suggest the minor rebellion in protected circumstances associated with college life: it is as if the garment as purchased, or even as tailored to the individual, is not quite correct and must be changed in some way by the individual to betoken a completely personal style without the artifice of a tailor or mom's alterations. Arrogant youth must determine its own style. Thus, chino shorts that lose little more than an inch in being rolled up are a far more powerful statement in that inch than if they were merely worn as purchased. The button-down shirt is not a collegiate invention, having been a style manufactured as early as 1901, according to Brooks Brothers, in adaption of the shirt with a fastened collar worn by polo players, but its imagery is compellingly collegiate. Much clothing that is collegiate is sanctioned as Ivy League style by such establishment stores as Brooks Brothers and J. Press and by catalog retailers such as L. L. Bean. In this land of the "haute" prep, the name Armani might never have been heard and torn jeans are scourged.

The route to the college market has often been circuitous. Loafers, after all, began as American Indian moccasins and traipsed to Norway and back again, finally to be sanctioned as appropriate collegiate dress. Young globetrotting Americans had discovered the soft shoes in Scandinavia in the 1930s, and although the specific design features were European, the concept was similar to that of the American Indian moccasin. Introduced by an American firm, G. H. Bass & Co., in 1936, the Bass Weejun (that is, Norwegian) penny loafer (denoting a fad at the time in which the coin was inserted in the "slot" of the vamp) became an American standard on campus by the 1940s. Chinos followed an even more unlikely trade route to reach the college campus: British India

James Stewart seems to have nes‑
tled into dormitory life on the m
Oxbridge of campuses in 1940; h
wears the indispensable Joe Col‑
lege wardrobe of the time: V-nec
pullover, cuffed trousers, cordov
penny loafers, and argyle socks.
His reading, also of the period, i
cludes Carl Sandburg's biograph
of Lincoln (1939), and his accom
plishments are discreetly an‑
nounced by a tennis trophy rathe
than a letter sweater.

*OPPOSITE: James Stewart. 1940. P
tographer: Eric Carpenter for MG.
Courtesy Wisconsin Center for Film a
Theater Research.*

Campus style was altered by the
return of veterans to college after
the Second World War, but certain
youthful classics remained, includ‑
ing, bottom left, cardigan sweat‑
ers, saddle shoes, and bow ties.
The history of the bow tie is un‑
deniably checkered, however. Al‑
though early in the century the
young Humphrey Bogart, above
right, aspired to collegiate smart‑
ness in bow tie and sweatshirt—
and of course the pipe of the cam‑
pus pacesetter—the bow tie was
by the 1950s, above left, a jaunty
deviation for a group of college stu‑
dents who gravitated toward the
ready-tied "$1.50 McKenzie"
model. In the 1980s the deliberate‑
ly *démodé* style would be revived
with social cachet only if the
youthful wearer could demonstrate
his mastery of tieing it himself. In
1986, Abbott Combes remarked in
The New York Times Magazine:
"Most men now wear bow ties be‑
cause most men don't." Only 3 to
5 percent of the neckties sold in
America that year were bow ties.

*Dickstein. ABOVE: Humphrey Bogart
age nineteen. c. 1918. Unknown phot
rapher for Warner Bros. Courtesy B
mann Archive.*

*TOP LEFT: Harvard students wearing the
McKenzie bow tie. Published in* Life,
New York, *June 18, 1951. Photographer:
Yale Joel. Courtesy Time Inc. BOTTOM
LEFT: American college couple. c. 1945.
Unknown photographer. Courtesy Sidney*

Men seldom wear furs except on that particularly animalistic occasion when viewing spectator sports on the college campus.

TOP: The Yell by John Held. Drawing published in The New York Times Magazine, January 16, 1954. Collection Addison Gallery of American Art, Phillips Academy. ABOVE: Man in a raccoon coat. 1915. Unknown photographer. Courtesy Smithsonian Institution. OPPOSITE The raccoon coat. Fashion editorial lished in Esquire, New York, Jan 1988. Photographer: Marcia Lippm Courtesy the photographer. OPPOS BOTTOM: Michael Stone at the Astor ber Shop. 1988. Photographer: Shanley. Courtesy the photographer.

exported its khaki cloth to China, and China sold it to Americans in the Philippines during the First World War; the Americans, not recognizing the variant on khaki, called the pants "chinos" because of their supposed Chinese origin. Most popular in the 1950s and 1960s, chinos lost ground on campus in the late 1960s and throughout the 1970s to the rival cotton pants, denim; since 1979, chinos have returned to the hallowed ivy halls. Chukka boots also originated among the British in India, but upon reaching America they were dubbed "desert boots," which gave them what may have seemed a more American flavor.

When Joe College assumed vast numbers and social suasion in the 1950s, his persona gave way to a specifically "Ivy League" look, which stressed the button-down collar and narrow tie, often knit and flat-bottomed, worn with the narrow-lapel suit. Soon this style that began as an exaggeration on campus became an epidemic as men long graduated sought association with the young and educated. In the 1970s when youth and education come to be taken for granted, the Joe College style

became even more nonchalant, with collars that flipped back and shirttails that hung below the sweater. Joe College in the 1980s returns to tradition—greatcoat, the dependable loafers, white socks, and a sweater with shirt collar protruding. His brusque collegiate self-assurance is emblematic of a generation. It also clearly reflects the enduring distinction that Joe College makes between the clothes of the world and the clothing of a budding individualist and his peers.

143

e life of the campus has its eter-
verities, including Oxford-cloth,
ton-down shirts, blazers, chi-
, corduroy pants, repp-striped
(either in four-in-hand or bow-
ormat), suede shoes, and loaf
Some insouciant undergradu-
eschewed socks in the 1970s
1980s. Lisa Birnbach in *The
cial Preppy Handbook* (1980)
onished men: "Go sockless.
ks are frequently not worn on
ting occasions or on social oc-
ons, for that matter. This pro-
s a year-round beachside look
is so desirable that comfort
be thrown aside." So perva-
was the trend that a young
's ankles might have been tak-
s the preppy erogenous zone.

SITE: *Preppies Sean-Patrick Carver
Geoff Scheumann in blazers. Pub-
d in* M, *New York, January 1988.
ographer: J. Cowley. Courtesy Fair-
Syndication.*

ral or conservative, the Joe
ege style survives the move to
political arena. More than the
of the blazer or the stripe of the
t is the manner of wearing
clothing. Even though John
nedy had lived in London as
of the Ambassador to the Court
James's, been Senator from
State of Massachusetts, and
d be the President of the
ed States, he wears the classic
ge wardrobe in the style of the
eague.

EFT: *Gary Hart supporter. c. 1983.
grapher: Abigail Heyman. Courtesy
ve Pictures Inc.* TOP RIGHT: *5th An-
Ice Cream Party of Congressional
er interns, Washington, D.C. 1987.
ographer: Keith McManus. Courtesy
ve Pictures Inc.* RIGHT: *John and
eline Kennedy at home. 1953. Pho-
her: Hy Peskin. Courtesy Staley-
Gallery.*

The undergraduate of 1940, and the graduate of 1967, opposite, reflect few changes in the Joe College imagery: the two outfits are virtually interchangeable across the generations. The young man above center may combine the propriety of a four-in-hand tie with the impropriety of beltless shorts and sockless sneakers, but these comminglings of style are viewed as adolescently beguiling in their disrespect and their traditionalism. In 1984–85, the yellow "power tie," seemingly admired for its brightness and suggestion of entrepreneurial spirit, briefly supplemented the young man's tie wardrobe of knits and repp stripes.

OPPOSITE: *Dustin Hoffman in* The Graduate. *1967. Unknown photographer for United Artists. Courtesy Kobal Collection.* LEFT: *James Stewart in classic Joe College garb. 1940. Unknown photographer for MGM. Courtesy Kobal Collection.* ABOVE CENTER: *Collegian at the Foxfield Race Course, Charlottesville, Virginia. Published in* M, *New York, July 1985. Photographer: George Chinsee. Courtesy Fairchild Syndication.* ABOVE RIGHT: *Young man at a Harvard University garden party. Published in* M, *New York, October 1985. Photograher: Victoria Gerwirtz. Courtesy Fairchild Syndication.*

THE BUSINESSMAN

The image of the businessman has been ameliorated from the limbo of cynicism and apparent avarice that it occupied in the nineteenth century to a more positive position in our own time. When George Bernard Shaw, in his early novel *Cashel Byron's Profession* (1882), referred to the businessman as one "who probably never read anything but a newspaper since he left school," his view of the industrialist as uncouth and unlettered was shared by most intellectuals (and gentlemen) of his time. The growing sophistication of industry and technology in the twentieth century has given the businessman a less unsavory image, even though vestiges of the Shavian notion remain. And business and the professions have unquestionably created standards of dress for the twentieth century.

According to John T. Molloy, the author of *Dress for Success* (1975), the suit "is the single most important garment that every man wears." He further referred to it as "the central power garment," thus giving it keystone status within the full array of men's clothing in the twentieth century. Evolving from the separate frock coat and trousers of the nineteenth century, the matched suit of the twentieth has become the expressive sign of the professional man. Whereas the laborer may have clothing directly related to his tasks, the suit of the businessman is the modern universal, a garment appropriate to the lawyer, the banker, the architect, and the present-day dealmaker. The butcher, the baker, and the candlestickmaker literally wear different hats, dressing in accordance with the specific needs of their professions; so, too, do the train engineer, the policeman, and the construction worker. But the chief executive officers of the railway, the municipal police agency, and the construction company will dress more or less alike, establishing their identities and their authoritative lines of power by means of the suit (even as the traveling salesman, in the 1920s and 1930s, sought professional recognition by wearing the available version of the garment). Denying distinctions among the professions, the suit dresses the professional elite and has traditionally been identified with its prestige and influence.

Ironically, it was not always so. In the nineteenth century, the black frock coat connoted supremacy, while the suit, in the prevalence of a single material throughout, was thought to be too much like a livery, or servant's uniform. Even today, it is not accidental that in French the man's suit is known as the *complet* (or in Italian, the *completo*), suggesting it to be attire that is complete or comprehensive but without individuality. In English, we know the suit to be "suitable," hence ever appropriate. The suit is the matrix of the modern man's wardrobe. In the 1980s, in the "About Men" column of *The New York Times Magazine*, Michael Korda advised: "The first rule is simple: Put your money into suits, not accessories. . . . If you want to get ahead, you should dress for success before you are a success. Different companies have different standards, and God knows, no subject produces more prejudices than men's clothes, but to my knowledge nobody objects to a dark-blue suit, a plain shirt, and a dark tie, so why give yourself more trouble than you need?" That this homily was offered in the 1980s and not in the decade of *The Man in the Gray Flannel Suit* (1955) testifies to the continuing and

financier and banker J. Pier-
Morgan, renowned for his re-
nization of major American
oads, founding of United
es Steel, and efforts in govern-
t financing from 1873 until his
h in 1913, was a patron of the
and a man of great personal
. From his handsomely pat-
ed foulard to his impressive
h fob, his attire supports his
ge as the man of power.

J. Pierpont Morgan, Esq. 1903.
ographer: Edward J. Steichen.
tesy The Metropolitan Museum of
The Alfred Stieglitz Collection, 1949.

...suasive affiliation of the suit with achievement. Moreover, the ...siness suit serves another function as well: it will pass, without ...ange, through all parts of the day, at least until a formal dinner or ...ening's entertainment demands other attire.

...The modern business suit stems from the late-1850s lounge coat, a ...ose, boxy jacket lacking the waist seam that defined the frock coat ...d its next of kin, the morning coat) of the period. The eminently ...nified but somewhat confining frock coat—shaped at the waist with ...attached skirt—was gradually supplanted by the freer comfort of the ...nge suit. The fabric of the early lounger was usually a tweed, cheviot, ...velvet, suggesting youth and informality. From this stylish fad would ...erge, by the mid-1860s, an ensemble with matched coat, waistcoat, ...d trousers, the forerunner of today's three-piece suit. Although the ...ck coat lost popularity, it still maintained its traditional authority for ...ne years. But by the end of the century, the lounge jacket, now of-...ed in a double-breasted style, was in the ascendant; in the same era, ...re formal fabrics were used, according to Cunnington, including ...rsteds, flannels (1892), and blue serge (1893), all materials that would ...come canonical suitings in the next century.

...Thus, with only minor variations, the lounge suit has become the ...entieth-century business suit. In a line of succession from the ...erican financier J. Pierpont Morgan (1837–1913) to the present, ...n of power have worn dark suits in a unified expression of authority. ...eir eminence is reinforced by the unadorned, all-business, no-non-...se suit of the century. Oil magnate John D. Rockefeller (1839–1937) ...pted the three-piece suit and set the style that would identify male ...stige until the Second World War. Even as professional classes ...pted the suit, it remained a nuanced privilege of the Establishment, ...distinctions depending not on differences of line but on the fabrics ...d details of fine tailoring learned by American haberdashers from ...ile Row. Ties and collars would vary—Morgan, in a 1903 Edward ...ichen photograph, would wear an octagon-pattern tie resembling an ...ot, whereas in 1941 the statesman Winston Churchill was photo-...phed by Karsh wearing a dotted bow tie—but the impact of the dark ...would abide. In mid-century Henry Luce (1898–1967), the founder ...he Time-Life publishing empire, would, like his predecessors in ...ver, wear a three-piece suit with watch chain and pocket square in ...manner of a mogul.

...Does one demonstrate the uniformity of the professions with this ...fessional uniform? Small variations have been allowed by some ...fessions, advertising often favoring a casual touch, such as a lighter ...or (the now-famous gray flannel, with the addition of a button-down-...ar shirt), and Wall Street preferring pinstripes. But the silhouette ...he suit remained uniform until the 1960s, when the great bifurcation ...ween "American" and "European" styles became pronounced. ...e high armholes, defined waist, larger lapels, and more substantial ...ulder padding of the European fitted suit was dramatically different ...n the American sack, the natural successor to the lounge suit. And ...European cut would give the sack suit a run for its money.

...he indomitable monolith of the business suit has largely gone un-...llenged in the twentieth century. Since the 1970s, as more and more ...men have assumed executive roles, they too have adopted modified ...sions of the man's business suit. Earlier, in the falling away from ...ss codes in the 1960s and thereafter, the suit or the jacket and tie were ...ndoned not by top executives but rather by clerks, tellers, and other ...eaucrats who were no longer required to dress to the professional ...dard—perhaps with the implication that they were unlikely to at-...professional status in any event. Although in looking at a group of ...inessmen from the 1920s (or from the 1950s), it may be difficult to ...inguish the most successful, some sixty years later the task is sim-...; the cut, fabrication, and accessories of the suit would surely betray ...social background—and perhaps the distinct profession—of the ...rer. In this sense, the assertion that the suit is the uniform of modern ...is only true in part. The suit is a nuanced and varied garment. Thus, ...n the two Presidential candidates Richard M. Nixon and John F. ...nedy met in 1960 before a national debate, the outcome of the ...test already seemed decided in the three-button suit of the more

Winston Churchill, in 1941 the Prime Minister of Great Britain, wears with dignity the dark three-piece suit, conservatively patterned tie, and gold watch fob so representative of British quality in dress. The motto of his people during the Second World War was "Business as usual!" American publisher Henry Luce, founder of the Time-Life empire, wears his three-piece suit and gold watch fob with the surety of style of one who has shaped opinion. He has what Egon von Furstenberg would call "the power look." In his book by the same name (1978), von Furstenberg noted that the power look "is a ticket to the winner's circle, a passport to the world where men enjoy privilege and pleasure, take command, and seem at ease everywhere."

OPPOSITE: *Winston Churchill. 1941. Photographer: Yousuf Karsh.* © *1941 Karsh, Ottawa. Courtesy Woodfin Camp & Associates.* BELOW: *Henry Luce. c. 1955. Photographer: Yousuf Karsh.* © *Karsh, Ottawa. Courtesy Woodfin Camp & Associates.*

With only minor variations in cut and fit, the suit as tailored at the beginning of the century has remained the standard for men's business attire to the present day. In 1900, American dramatist William Clyde Fitch, author of a popular play about the dandy Beau Brummell, wears a three-piece suit that differs little from the one worn by the young Anthony J. Drexel Biddle, Jr., a dozen years later. Today as in 1910, classic materials are the stuff of men's suits, and the most desired effect is to look as if one had dressed to a generation before. The one element of business attire that has changed radically since the first decade of the century is the collar, which is no longer the stiff, starched variety worn by Thomas M. Osborne and his sons.

Businessmen in groups seem to seek homogeneity in their suits and overcoats and individuality only in such specific details as tie, collar treatments, and possibly the selection of a two- rather than three-piece suit.

ABOVE: Group of American businessmen, c. 1928. Unknown photographer. Courtesy Bettmann Archive. OPPOSITE: Commuters, Park Forest, Illinois. 19-. Photographer: Dan Weiner. Courtesy Mrs. Dan Weiner.

TOP LEFT: William Clyde Fitch. c.1900. Photographer: Pach Brothers. Courtesy The New-York Historical Society. CENTER LEFT: Anthony J. Drexel Biddle, Jr., and his wife, Mary Duke Biddle. c. 1912. Unknown photographer. Courtesy Library of Congress. BOTTOM LEFT: Penologist Thomas M. Osborne with his sons. c. 1910. Unknown photographer. Courtesy Library of Congress.

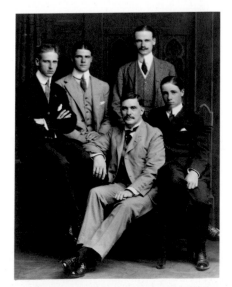

Many have argued that the 1960 American Presidential election was won by John F. Kennedy on the basis of the first nationally televised debate between candidates. More forceful and confident than Richard M. Nixon, Kennedy may have won on intellectual grounds alone, but perhaps it was his dark suit and fine tailoring that actually elected him President. Later, when Kennedy was in office, he was asked to pose for the magazine *Gentlemen's Quarterly*, and he wryly remarked that there was something cynical about having his Presidential achievements represented in a moment as a male model.

BELOW: Senator John F. Kennedy and Vice President Richard M. Nixon meet just before their first nationally televised debate. September 26, 1960. Unknown photographer. Courtesy Bettmann Archive.

conservative candidate compared with the looser, two-button suit of th liberal. In the movie *Wall Street* (1987), the corporate raider Gordo Gekko (played by Michael Douglas) advises his protégé to see his tail in order to dress the part.

When the military man returned from the Second World War, th American consolidation of power and enterprise was represented by th businessman's suit. A war and a world won, the American triumph w dressed in a two-piece suit, its functionalism the heritage of America ingenuity and its symbolism laden with commerce and technolog Capable of a mass production on the model of military clothing, the su was a sign of America's success and of the businessman's achievement.

In 1955, the Sloan Wilson novel *The Man in the Gray Flannel Suit* seize the imagination of a generation of readers. A best seller in its time ar translated into dozens of languages, it was the subject of a popular mov in 1956. *The Man in the Gray Flannel Suit* is a morality tale whose lesse remains pertinent today, even as its plot had become all but lost memory. The metaphor of the suit remains: it represents conformi and a means to business success.

The protagonist of the novel is Tom Rath, an army veteran and a li able guy, who enters the world of public relations in order to make mo money for himself, his wife, and his three children. When Tom's bc asks for his opinion about a speech, Tom wonders whether he shou be truthful or not. He says to himself: "I should quit if I don't like wh he does, but I want to eat, and so, like a half millon other guys in gra flannel suits, I'll always pretend to agree, until I get big enough to honest without being hurt. That's not being crooked, it's just bei smart." If Tom Rath were to act on this cynicism, he would become number in the gray-flannel ranks, but he does not. Instead, he tells t boss the speech is bad and the boss accepts his candor and offers hir new and better assignment. Tom neither capitulates nor conforms, a nonetheless enjoys a kind of success. Thus, the man in the gray-flann suit can, according to Wilson, act heroically and individually even as acknowledges that his life and attire are threatened by the powere forces that suppress moral dignity and decision. The protagonist, Tc Rath, sought and discovered profound purposes in his life even as wore a costume he associated with lesser, and less clarified, values.

In contrast, the bedrock of John Molloy's cynical prescription is t suit. For Molloy, it represents the most serious part of the wardrobe a a significant investment for the male. It would serve to establish cc formity and thereby initiate traits necessary for success. Molloy mal of the suit a suborned uniform and a sign of conformity, a means identify with success in business and an element to be manipulate Molloy's style paradigm is only contrivance and opportunism.

Sloan Wilson sustained the concept of the suit as a metaphor for modern businessman. His particular interpretation was important in 1950s, and it is important today. His metaphor abides because it is c of the most persuasive and trenchant understandings of modern m: The suit is the businessman whole cloth, as it were.

The suit as metaphor for modern man was the subject of the popular novel and film *The Man in the Gray Flannel Suit* (in 1955 and 1956, respectively). Growing out of the postwar concern for the seemingly excessive conformity of the American male, the thesis was based on such formulations as that of sociologist David Reisman, in *Individualism Reconsidered* (1954), who wrote of the need to "give every encouragement to people to develop their private selves—to escape from groupism." The uniform of the businessman of that era was the two- or three-button suit with lightly padded shoulders, a silhouette that came to be called "American."

OPPOSITE: Gregory Peck in The Man in the Gray Flannel Suit. *1956. Unknown photographer for Twentieth Century Fox. Courtesy Kobal Collection. INSET: Advertisement for a Hart Schaffner & Marx gray-flannel suit. 1952. Unknown photographer. Courtesy Hartmarx Corporation, Chicago.*

The traditional suit followed the fortunes of the Nixon Presidency in the 1970s. The attire of White House Counsel John Dean, testifying before the Congressional hearings on Watergate in 1973, has the established rectitude of the business suit, but displays a certain lack of distinction and quality.

LEFT: John Dean. 1973. Photographer: Mark Godfrey. Courtesy Archive Pictures Inc.

Wall Street is the special bastion of the suit in America. Although casual styles have affected many professions since the rebellious years of the 1970s, the suit constitutes the metaphorical armor for the financial battle on Wall Street.

LEFT, RIGHT, AND BOTTOM RIGHT: Wall Street Style. Published in M, New York, January 1985. Photographer: Amy Meadow. Courtesy Fairchild Syndication.

The styles of the film *Wall Street* (1987) were created by American designer Alan Flusser, whose tailoring is more British than the British. His conception of the dress of fast-lane finance is perhaps only an intensification of the actual dress of the place. In London, a young British trader wears suspenders—or, as he would call them, braces—which were revived in the 1980s. Beset by unfavorable press for its association with junk bonds and certain unsavory practices, the world of finance perhaps revived the most traditional dress—worn with elan by Gary Cooper—to offset its new image.

ABOVE LEFT: Michael Douglas as Gordon Gekko in Wall Street. *1987. Unknown photographer for Twentieth Century Fox. Courtesy Kobal Collection. ABOVE RIGHT: Anthony Mulliner in the trading room of Scrimgeour Vickers and Co., London. Published in* M, *New York, October 1986. Photographer: Tim Jenkins. Courtesy Fairchild Syndication. LEFT: Gary Cooper. 1931. Photographer: E. R. Richee for Paramount Pictures. Courtesy Kobal Collection.*

No Matter How Well You Dress,

Shearson Lehman Brothers Inc.
New York, N.Y.

The revelation that Wall Streeters from a conservative investment firm might wear jeans concerns both clothing and style. The stolidity of the corporate appearance is contrasted with the free play of individual personalities in jeans. For all intents and purposes, the contrast is between the dispassionate and the passionate, or personal.

ABOVE AND OPPOSITE: "No matter how well you dress . . . There's always room for improvement." 1987. Advertisement for Levi's Special Reserve Jeans. Photographer: Richard Avedon. Courtesy Levi Strauss & Co.

THERE'S ALWAYS ROOM FOR IMPROVEMENT.

LEVI'S SPECIAL RESERVE JEANS

THE MAN ABOUT TOWN

Impeccable, conservative (as evidenced by his wing collar), but consistently high style, actor William Powell played countless Hollywood roles as the man about town. Cast above as the dapper, ever-elegant detective Philo Vance, he would play the part in a number of movies between 1929 and 1933.

ABOVE: William Powell. 1929. Unknown photographer for Paramount Pictures. Courtesy Bettmann Archive.

Adding to the unflinching paradox of being a modern executive who collects Victoriana, publisher Christopher Forbes, opposite, wears the anachronistic wing collar with business dress.

OPPOSITE: Christopher Forbes. Published in Uomo Harper's Bazaar, *Milan, Fall–Winter 1982–83. Photographer: Alex Chatelain. Courtesy Edizioni Syds-Italia s.r.l.*

"It is important not to let the public have a loophole to lampoon you. . . I myself dearly love a good match, yet I know it is overdoing to wear socks, and handkerchief of the same color. I take ruthless stock of mys in the mirror before going out. A polo jumper or unfortunate tie expo one to danger."—Noel Coward, in *Cecil Beaton's Diaries, 1922–1939*, 19

The man about town is a figure whose image is one of elegance a style. His adherence to standards of beauty and taste is resolute, a his attention to the details of dress are without parallel. The operat word is elegance, but its definition may alter with classes, generatio and social circumstances. Although royal birth is not a requisite for man about town, many of the attributes by which he is known were fined in the 1920s and 1930s by Edward, Prince of Wales. The fut Edward VIII (King of Great Britain and Northern Ireland), he reign only a year, in 1936, thereafter to be designated the Duke of Winds

Even in the early years of his public life, in the 1920s, the Princ Wales would dress in a manner of personal command. Whether in o man's tank top, military trench coat, or golfer's knickers and Fair sweater, he was a man of style. But it was in formal portraits of the 19 that his urbanity became most apparent. When photographed by C Beaton in 1936, he was a dashing figure in the crisp tailoring of Sav Row, self-confident and utterly at ease, lending an air of informalit the occasion, a trait to be admired by any man about town. As impo ably attired in a George Hoyningen-Huene portrait a year later, combined a formal business suit with the suave touches of a striped d shirt and dotted tie. Ever the style setter and ever comfortable with style, the Duke of Windsor, as he was then known, seemed to d correctly on any occasion. Throughout his life, his demand for patt and pattern mix was insatiable, and from the 1930s onward, his la full knotting of the necktie—in the famous Windsor knot—create formidable style that would endure. From his choice of cuffed trou for his plaid suits to his preference for soft white shirts with black he was, until his death in 1972, a style leader and the quintessential about town.

The choice of collar and tie is an important aspect of dress for the about town. The pairing of a spread collar with a wide tie or of a nar four-in-hand with a collar having long points may be one of his characteristic style gestures, especially as these items of neckwear not part of the body but rather frame the face. Thus, in a 1929 ph graph of the film star William Powell, posed with gloves in hand a Homburg on his head, the most salient aspect of the actor's image i mating of the wing collar with a bow tie. The wing (the high, stiff c with pointed ends, which turn down), already an anachronism Powell's day, is worn by publisher Christopher Forbes in 1982, and style is at an even further remove from the present; in manner, howe it seems timeless, in keeping with the style of the man about town, selects his tie and collar from any period out of supreme personal p erence. Moreover, Forbes does not even equivocate with a bow which was still compatible with the wing collar in the 1980s; rathe

elects to wear a four-in-hand. This determined historicist gesture is, a sense, appropriate to the collar, for this style of tie was only assigne its traditional role at the beginning of the twentieth century. Since th the four-in-hand tie (named for the way in which it is knotted, like t reins held by the driver of the four-in-hand carriage) has undergon transformation from its more effulgent origins to the slimmed-dov version we know today.

In a famous Edward Steichen photograph of 1930, the young Ga Cooper, then beginning to play leading roles in films, wears a shirt wi an extremely long collar, on which the tips are bending up instead pointing down. Although eminently debonair, Cooper was caught b tween the relatively new attached collar (which is not as stiff as t heavily starched detachable collar had been) and the creation of t Windsor knot later in the decade. Nevertheless, his collar is comp mented by the peaked lapels of his jacket, thus fostering a consonar between two extremes of clothing, which when mated are harmonious

One of Hollywood's most self-assured men about town was Fred A taire, whose magical creative talent on the dance floor was coupled w a personal sartorial grace. In a 1936 portrait, Astaire makes his selecti of a collar with great care, for he wears a collar pin that accentuates closure of the collar points and the narrowness of the knot of the tie. L the Duke of Windsor, Astaire favored the mixing of patterns, in this stance adopting a striped shirt and dotted tie, although neither co nor tie is like those preferred by the Duke of Windsor in the same riod. The collar pin, of no structural necessity except to hug the co to the tie, provides a flash of jewelry for the man about town. The R erend Adam Clayton Powell, Jr., a man of the cloth as well as a n about town (and, indeed, a Congressman from New York's Harl for some thirty years), wore a collar pin in the same manner as trimmed his mustache, that is, with an irreproachable but slightly pa correctness. None of these men about town wears the tab-collar dr shirt, the favored style of the Duke of Windsor, who, it is said, fou the joined tabs of the shirt the appropriate channel for the tie.

The man about town seems to have had a particular affinity for double-breasted suit. There is a redolence of another time and anot place about the style, as if to suggest that this suit, while only margin acceptable for business, is slightly more stylish than the more pop single-breasted style. Although the double-breasted suit had preva in the nineteenth century, the widespread popularity of the figu disguising, single-breasted sack suit in the early years of the twenti established it as this century's preeminent style. The double-breas suit achieved style supremacy in the 1930s and 1980s, however. In e decade, there had been a firm association with the past; in the 19 it had been consciously revived in emulation of the forms of some f years before. In the 1980s, the revival was spearheaded by Giorgio mani and other Italian designers, who liberally quoted the styles of 1930s and saw them as images to be taken forward fifty years once ag The issue for the man about town, then, was a matter of making a sonal selection, never succumbing to popular taste but followir slightly idiosyncratic sartorial bent; never making himself subjec reproach but not relying on common wisdom, either.

And the advice of common wisdom is clear. Today, when the bc on dressing for success advise a young man to buy his first suit, t never suggest the double-breasted style; he is advised to acquire only if his wardrobe has been fully stocked with more "appropri office attire. In going against the grain, there is a volition to style an attempt to associate oneself with wealth and extravagance.

In the 1930s, Clark Gable and other men of Hollywood wore dou breasted suits with an authority and elegance that might exceed protocols of most business offices. Indeed, the style reached boardroom in that era; and although history may offer another ratior it was film and such figures as Cary Grant who provided the extra agery. Even though British tailors in that era called it the lounge s suggesting its transition from the nineteenth-century world of exclu private clubs to public lounges where less aristocratic men would gregate, elegant men such as the playwright Eugene O'Neill and c poser Cole Porter would happily wear the double-breasted suit, O'

Elevated to the British throne in 1936, Edward VIII would abdicate at year's end to marry Wallis Simpson, and he was named the Duke of Windsor at their marriage the following year. In this Cecil Beaton portrait, above, King Edward displays the sovereignty of British tailoring in his well-cut, double-breasted suit with a trace of silk emerging from the pocket.

ABOVE: King Edward VIII. 1936. Photographer: Cecil Beaton. Courtesy Sotheby's, London.

ch a rumpled defiant nonchalance. The double-breasted suit re-
rned in the 1980s with avatars of personal style. Again, Hollywood
s instrumental in the move, as young film stars incorporated the ex-
nsive, casual look of American designers, a touch of street style, and
etrograde, history-aware, Italian high style into their dress.

Pattern is a further prerogative of the man about town. His choices
materials and designs have been more adventuresome than those of
e businessman, and his ability to mix them is without predestination
conventions of taste. Thus poet Jean Cocteau and composer Noel
ward consorted their checks, plaids, and polka dots in emphatic
mbinations that seemed both bold and mysterious and called atten-
n to the detail of their clothes. Likewise, Baron Nicolas de Gunzberg
d Sir Anthony Eden adopted pattern in the form of bold stripes for
eir portraits of 1934 and 1951.

A reactionary wardrobe refinement for the man about town is the
istcoat or vest, early in the century worn by Rudolph Valentino and
lliam Kissam Vanderbilt in a decorative fabric to soften the effect of
suit. Although the idea seems to have anticipated the Peacock
volution of the 1960s, it was historically located in the nineteenth
tury, when waistcoats not only provided warmth but also introduced
unmatched element into the outfit, giving the wardrobe variation
style. Tattersall, geometric, and other decorative motifs appeared
waistcoats of the era; in the 1980s, a cardigan sweater would serve
knit version of the vest, as in the working costume of the photog-
her Horst.

Dapper by day, the man about town becomes a sophisticate at night,
r adjusting his wardrobe one notch above the standard and one notch
k into history. When the bureaucrat and the bourgeois wear black
the man about town wears white, relishing its *démodé* formality.
at many of the man-about-town exemplars are entertainers is logical,
they have a natural association with night life and the sybaritic, daz-
g world of café society. Thus, in the 1930s, actors with the shining
d looks of Tyrone Power, Maurice Chevalier, and Franchot Tone
e associated with the swallowtail coat, white piqué vest, and wing
ar with white tie in the black-and-white composition that evening
ar offers for men. Even out of white tie, Koval's 1927 evening ele-
ce was the ideal of the café-society habitué, and in the 1960s, the
te dinner jacket of James Bond restores the empire to Britain that
d nearly lost.

o the man about town belongs the tuxedo, a fundamental element
is wardrobe of the evening. White tie and tails may have been the
ored form of dress for true sophisticates in the 1930s, but the tuxedo
waiting in the wings. It has a specific date and place of origin. In
6, a man named Griswold Lorillard wore a smoking jacket to the
umn Ball at the aristocratic Tuxedo Park Club in Orange County,
v York, and his inspired impudence and improvisation were the start
long tradition. In time, the tuxedo, as the jacket came to be called,
ld virtually replace the tailcoat on formal occasions. What the tux-
offered, in addition to its associations with Tuxedo Park, was a
fortable, adaptable formal style, succeeding because of its sim-
ity. In its purest, most dashing form, it is black with white accents,
ern, Puritan, even ministerial expression of style. Although Loril-
's first outing was in color—and pastels and other colors have wan-
ed in and out of the tuxedo's realm in the intervening years—this
der was banished as quickly as the hoi polloi from the property of
Tuxedo Park Club. The tuxedo complements the formally dressed
an; she is the coloristic, creative center of attention, while the man
ds by her side in unqualified and unmitigated good taste. There is
ty and sanctuary in the tuxedo and the certainty that "everyone"
s good in one.

o be sure, this is not the case, but the simplicity of dress offered by
style is highly seductive. Almost everyone, male or female, looks
ndid in simple combinations of black and white, especially when
white is assuredly fresh and and the black is richly textured. The
mony of the tuxedo's black-and-white composition has sometimes
e sour when a constituent element has been appropriated in recent
s. For example, the pleated-front tuxedo shirt (in synthetic fabrics)

More than a man about town, the
Duke of Windsor was a man of the
world and a man of style. Photographed with the Duchess of
Windsor in 1947, he wears a suit
of twilled fabric and a shirt with
spread collar, a style he had adopted early in life.

ABOVE: *The Duke and Duchess of Windsor. 1947. Cover of* Life, *May 22,
1950. Photographer: Philippe Halsman.
© 1989 Yvonne Halsman.*

Continued on page 174

163

The Windsor knot, wide in girth
and worn with spread-collar shirts,
took its name from the way the
Duke of Windsor knotted his tie,
above left. Thirty years earlier,
photographed by George Hoyningen-Huene, above, he wore a dotted tie with a striped shirt in one
of his more subdued pattern
mixtures.

*TOP LEFT: The Duke of Windsor. 1967.
Photographer: Patrick Lichfield. Courtesy
the photographer. ABOVE: The Duke of
Windsor. 1937. Photographer: George
Hoyningen-Huene. Courtesy Staley-Wise
Gallery.*

Two men of Hollywood dominating men's style in the 1930s were Fred Astaire and Gary Cooper. Their collars are extreme, in one case narrowed by a collar pin and in the other having elongated tips. The debonair Adam Clayton Powell, Jr., a leading man in politics, also wore his collar pinned. Traditionally, young men are found to wear collars that rise low and direct attention to the neck; older men with wrinkled necks are advised to wear high collars to minimize the visible expanse. By this logic, high collars are associated with older men and tradition; low collars and special treatments are associated with the young.

TOP LEFT: Fred Astaire. c. 1936. Photographer: Laszlo Willinger. Courtesy Staley-Wise Gallery. BOTTOM LEFT: Gary Cooper. 1930. Photographer: Edward Steichen. Courtesy Staley-Wise Gallery. TOP RIGHT: Adam Clayton Powell, Jr. c. 1945. Unknown photographer. Courtesy Library of Congress.

The double-breasted suit and a thickly knotted tie are mated with panache by film star Cary Grant, left, and composer Cole Porter, above. Clark Gable, opposite, wears a three-piece suit, single-breasted but with the peaked lapels customarily associated with the double-breasted style, their edges hand-picked. Among the suit's other fine finishing touches are carefully executed besom pockets, on which a fold of fabric stitched at top and bottom.

LEFT: Cary Grant. 1943. Unknown photographer. ABOVE: Cole Porter. 19.. Photographer: Horst. Courtesy the photographer. OPPOSITE: Clark Gable 1933. Photographer: George Hurrell, MGM. Courtesy Kobal Collection.

The repertory of patterns for the man about town, beginning in the 1920s and extending into the 1940s, included stripes, tonal mixtures, and variations on the glen plaid too unorthodox for the businessman but appropriate, nevertheless, for the more seductive, artistic—not to mention narcissistic—man about town.

OPPOSITE: Cary Grant. 1945. Unknown photographer for Columbia Pictures. Courtesy Kobal Collection. TOP LEFT: Eugene O'Neill. Late 1920s. Unknown photographer. Courtesy Bettmann Archive. BOTTOM RIGHT: Gary Cooper. 1938. Unknown photographer for Paramount Pictures. Courtesy Kobal Collection.

Whether at the peak of fastidiousness or the edge of arrogance, the gestures of French poet, playwright, and novelist Jean Cocteau included the self-conscious mixing of patterns and the display of unbuttoned, turned-up cuffs and oppositional stripes.

OPPOSITE: Jean Cocteau. 1949. Photographer: Yousuf Karsh. © Karsh, Ottawa. Courtesy Woodfin Camp & Associates. ABOVE: Jean Cocteau. c. 1937. Photographer: Raymond Voinquel. © 1989 Raymond Voinquel, Paris.

Boldness of pattern and its mix distinguish the stylish man about town, a distinction here reinforced by pose and deportment. In the images of Noel Coward, above right and opposite, and of Baron Nicolas de Gunzberg, above left, the air of Renaissance kit-kat portraiture lingers, revealing hands as well as face and bust to create a portrait without fault or falter.

ABOVE LEFT: Baron Nicolas de Gunzberg. 1934. Photographer: Horst. Courtesy the photographer. ABOVE RIGHT: Noel Coward. 1935. Photographer: Horst. Courtesy the photographer. OPPOSITE: Noel Coward. 1943. Photographer: Cecil Beaton. Courtesy Sotheby's, London.

was popular in the early 1970s as a casual style for wear with jeans, t
when removed from its original ensemble, it lost its dignity—the p
separated from the whole became a mockery.

Even as the soft bow tie has become an uncommon feature of bu
ness dress, its place in evening wear is assured because of the flour
with which it sets off the formal collar. In black silk, the bow tie is raki
a fitting device for a gentleman. Black tie, its description now a syn
doche for the entire evening ensemble, is essential in contempor.
formal wear in order to distinguish it from clerical wear—giving t
collar a twist and flair unlike any we would expect a minister to wea

There have been indignities to the tuxedo, of course, including
countless excesses of boys and bands in high school proms and croupi
in Las Vegas casinos, but these have had relatively little impact in
world still governed by the elite of Tuxedo Park. In the 1960s, L
Snowdon introduced the Nehru jacket as tuxedo (an ingenious inve
tion of brief duration), and Lyndon Baines Johnson, true to his Te
informality, required a Presidential inauguration in black tie rather th
the customary white. But essentially the story of the tuxedo is one
constraint and convention. Born of Lorillard's "preppy" rebellion,
dinner jacket and its ensemble are not only the style of the Tuxedo P
gritted-teeth aristocrats. Legend has it, as New York clothier P
Stuart reminded us in a 1980s advertisement, that Benjamin Gugg
heim, heir to the metals fortune, prepared for all exigencies when
sailed on the *Titanic* in 1912. On being told the ship was sinking, G
genheim retired to his cabin with his valet and reappeared on deck
formal dress, complete with diamond studs and cufflinks. If heaven
to be his destination, he clearly wanted to arrive properly dressed. L
Guggenheim, countless men in this century have followed their reso
to dress for the occasion. The sale of tuxedos increased rapidly in
1980s as more and more men found occasion to wear them. And
tuxedo has gone beyond the world of the *Titanic* and Tuxedo Pa
"The Three Diors" advertising campaign for Christian Dior, crea
by Doon Arbus and photographer Richard Avedon in 1982–83, sir
lated a Noel Coward world of elegance and joyous living and stimula
countless men to investigate the mysteries of black tie.

The dressing gown, or smoking jacket, is the at-home garment of
ever-elegant man about town. It is closely related to the tuxedo, f
is in fact the garment that Griswold Lorillard was wearing in 1886.
as much the style possession of the man about town as any detai
grooming or deportment. In the history of costume, its source is
banyan, the eighteenth-century gown of the English gentleman at
sure. The dressing gown was worn with both collar and tie in the quil
satin version of illustrator J. C. Leyendecker (in an Arrow Collar
vertisement of 1913). On the darker side of sensuality, men in
dressing gowns (and their synthetic semblances) have possessed
popular power of the seducer, whether the suave John Gilbert (p
tographed in 1927), Playboy Club *capo* Hugh Hefner (1984), or
artistic *capo* Julian Schnabel (1984).

The man about town indulges himself in historicism in clothing
style, reaching back to earlier times to justify what may often seer
be idiosyncratic styles for this artistically tinged boulevardier of the
order, ever attired with the finesse of the old. One step ahead, one
behind, and one cut above conventionality, the man about town
conspicuous and self-confident man.

Sir Anthony Eden, British statesman and a conspicuous figure on
best-dressed lists in America,
earned his fashion role by combining the most traditional clothing
with adventuresome details of
style and pattern.

ABOVE: Anthony Eden. Published in
Life, *New York, November 12, 1951.*
Photographer: Alfred Eisenstaedt. Cour-
tesy Time Inc.

The photographer Horst creates a self-portrait with an inventive assembly of style components that are by convention incompatible, including web belt, dark suit, loose tie, and sweater vest.

BELOW: Self-Portrait. 1985. Photographer: Horst. Courtesy the photographer.

y in the century, the man
t town might have worn a vest
contrasting fabric, Rudolph
ntino, above, choosing a cot-
piqué waistcoat to combine
the stripes of his shirt and suit
William Kissam Vanderbilt,
r right, a pronounced tatter-
attern to mitigate the severity
frock coat.

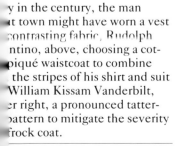

The Duke of Windsor was often the agent of fashion change. Preferring soft shirts and standard spread collars in formal dress, he challenged the convention of wearing the stiff, piqué shirt with white tie. But the stiffness of the white shirt when worn with white or black tie resisted even the provocation of the preeminent style figure of the century, and it remained an option in evening wear.

ABOVE: Baron Adolphe de Meyer. 1932. Photographer: George Hoyningen-Huene. Courtesy Harvard Theatre Collection. TOP RIGHT: Maurice Chevalier. 1925. Photographer: James Abbe. © 1989 Kathryn Abbe. Courtesy Staley-Wise Gallery. CENTER RIGHT: Nils Asther. 1929. Photographer: Ruth Harriet Louise for MGM. Courtesy Wisconsin Center for Film and Theater Research. BOTTOM RIGHT: Franchot Tone. 1933. Photographer: George Hurrell for MGM. Courtesy Wisconsin Center for Film and Theater Research. OPPOSITE TOP: Tyrone Power. 1938. Photographer: Laszlo Willinger. Courtesy Kobal Collection and Staley-Wise Gallery. OPPOSITE BOTTOM: Koval. 1927. Photographer: George Hoyningen-Huene. Courtesy Harvard Theatre Collection.

They loved armadillos, the American flag, and they disliked all their friends equally.

Dior Women's Sportswear

Women's Jewelry. Men's Dress Shirts. Neckwear, Accessories and Formal Wear.

Christian Dior

A government agent dressed to kill and the chic Diors dressed to the nines represent the tuxedo as the natural attire of those who move gracefully into the evening hours from the adventure—or the drawing-room comedy—of daily life.

LEFT: "The Three Diors." 1982. Advertisement for Christian Dior. Photographer: Richard Avedon. Courtesy Richard Avedon Studio and Christian Dior Inc. ABOVE: Sean Connery as James Bond in Goldfinger. *1964. Unknown photographer for United Artists. Courtesy Kobal Collection.*

Wondrously differentiated from the legion of men in rented evening clothes, artist Richard Merkin, on the page following, wears a double-breasted tuxedo with a wide shawl collar reminiscent of styles from the 1930s, complementing it by adding a satin-striped jacquard bow tie with a soft shirt.

FOLLOWING PAGE: Richard Merkin. Fashion editorial published in Uomo Harper's Bazaar, *Milan, Fall–Winter 1982–83. Photographer: Alex Chatelain. Courtesy Edizioni Syds-Italia s.r.l.*

The dressing gown, a sign of near dandyism and of affluent leisured evenings, derives from the banyan, the flowing gown of the eighteenth-century Hindu merchant. With his taste for exotic materials, he often lined the robe with a contrasting fabric so that it could be worn either side out. As the at-home attire of the man about town, the dressing gown could be interpreted as the riotously patterned banyan of Sacheverell Sitwell or the quietly elegant silk robe of actor John Gilbert. The emphasis throughout is on exquisite fabrics and fine detailing.

TOP LEFT: William Powell in The Benson Murder Case. *1930. Unknown photographer for Paramount Pictures. Courtesy Bettmann Archive. CENTER LEFT: Advertisement for Arrow Collar by J. C. Leyendecker. 1913. Courtesy Michael Schau. CENTER RIGHT: Sacheverell Sitwell. 1927. Photographer: Cecil Beaton. Courtesy Sotheby's, London. LEFT: John Gilbert. 1927. Photographer: Ruth Harriet Louise. Courtesy Kobal Collection.*

Oh those Diors, with minds instead of muscles and nothing up their sleeves, you just had to love them.

Dior Women's Intimates and Jewelry

Women's Legwear and Footwear.
Men's Robes, Dress Shirts, Neckwear,
Accessories, Hosiery and Formal Wear.
Dioressence and Eau Sauvage.

Christian Dior

Rococo love play transplants the elegant dressing gown to the drawing room as an amusing company known as "the three Diors," brought together for an advertising campaign, reconstitutes the 1930s with the mores of the 1980s. Another *ménage à trois*, one in dressing gown, elaborates the complex and changing affections of the world of Brideshead, the country home invented by Evelyn Waugh for his novel *Brideshead Revisited* (1945) and brought to life in a British television series of the same name in 1981.

LEFT: "The Three Diors." 1982. Advertisement for Christian Dior. Photographer: Richard Avedon. Courtesy Richard Avedon Studio and Christian Dior Inc. ABOVE: Jeremy Irons, Anthony Andrews, and Diana Quick in the television series "Brideshead Revisited." 1981. Unknown photographer for Granada. Courtesy Kobal Collection.

Two new emperors wear the silk robe with a black T-shirt or a pair of silk pajamas, giving a sinister cast to these partners of Venus and of Athena's helmet. Most silk dressing gowns are now made from a foulard fabric, which features a satin surface and a small, geometric repeat pattern made popular in men's neckwear.

LEFT: Julian Schnabel. 1984. Photographer: Jeannette Barron. Courtesy Staley-Wise Gallery. RIGHT: Hugh Hefner and Carrie Leigh. 1984. Photographer: Helmut Newton. Courtesy the photographer.

Ribald seduction became the prime motif of the shaving coat of the 1970s, a kimono-inflected garment in terrycloth and velour.

On the page opposite, the sumptuous play of textures for the man of luxury at home includes soft wool, elegant thick flannel, and silk paisley that is transferred from the nineteenth-century woman's woolen shawl.

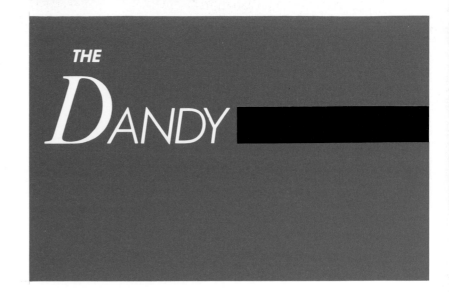

THE DANDY

The dandy has been amply dressed in history and literature. As described by Thomas Carlyle in *Sartor Resartus* (1833–34), he is "a man whose trade, office and existence consists in the wearing of Clothes. Every faculty of his soul, spirit, purse, and person is heroically consecrated to the wearing of Clothes wisely and well: so that as others dress to live, he lives to dress." The dandy of Carlyle and other nineteenth-century observers of the species is alive today. At times he may be identified as such, at others he may be viewed as a fashion victim; and occasionally he may even be seen as a style pacesetter. The pace may be a rapid regression into the past or a progression into the future. More important is its succession into the self. The narcissistic self-awareness of the dandy distinguishes him from the man about town not by intention but by degree. The dandy is ever an extreme form.

The contemporary artists David McDermott and Peter McGough take on the historical styles of the dandy in their art as in their lives. Their personal identification with a dandy and his time extends not only to the appropriation of his artistic style but also to the simulation of his lifestyle, as if they had been born in an earlier time. The evocation of historical styles is similarly carried out in fashion stylizations that seek exemplars in history. Thus, pre-Raphaelite stillness and an even more distant past are suggested in Lord Snowdon's 1987 portrait of Hamish Bowles, the British fashion journalist. The contemporary model assumes a world-weary pose and mien in clothing redolent of the past. Indeed, for the dandy, clothing is but an accessory to his self-image, not the most important part of his image-making. As important as dress may be, it is only the physical component of a nearly spiritual state. The eighteenth-century man of fashion Beau Brummell remained a dandy in disposition long after he was subjected to poverty and degradation. Brummell is said to have spent hours every morning in a ritual grooming that included a bath in milk; he was so meticulous in his dress that even the soles of his shoes were polished. The devices of the dandy, then, are not so much directed to the discrete elements of his dress as to an approach to dressing, often shared with other men of style, but ultimately reaching a narcissistic and personal definition.

The dandy in historical regression most often directs his attention to those periods in history that provide a great wealth of aesthetic ideas. It is not clothing that is the grail but the fulfillment of a personal aesthetic vision of history. Thus, the inspiration of Vienna and its riding elegance, its capital-city hegemony, and its artistic leadership gives license to create an artistic style that is not pure Viennese but rather a conflation of the imagery of writer Robert Musil (in his descriptions, tinged with melancholy, of the Hapsburg Empire in decline) and the languorous aestheticism of the artist Egon Schiele. Youth plays a significant part in the dandy aspiration (an irony, since it would seem to obtain as a lifetime disposition). The contemporary ideal of the English dandy may be Evelyn Waugh's young Sebastian Flyte, the Oxford aesthete of *Brideshead Revisited* (1945), redolent of genteel socialism, Establishment provocation, androgyny, and contemplative self-absorption. And if the dandy is aesthetic and self-concerned, his natural affiliation with professions is only with the poet, the artist, or the writer.

Even as swinging London of the 1960s simulated the dandy and propelled him into a larger realm, his style emulated the eighteenth-century poet or the exotic nineteenth-century aesthete compounded of a North African-European connection. The personal idiosyncracies and narcissism of a dandy perhaps compel him to identify not with a single figure in history but with the sense of an era or a place. At the end of the last century, Comte Robert de Montesquiou, the Paris dandy, avoided a meeting with Oscar Wilde, his contemporary and counterpart in London: one dandy does not emulate another, so self-conscious is he about the creation of his own identity, a process as well as a realization. So infused is the dandy with the past that a monocle, suggestive but not indicative, or a puffy four-in-hand tie may be enough to establish a historical assocation. In coiffure, the tousled hair of the would-be poet may be enough to establish a link to the Romantics, then confirmed in the wearing of collars of perverse complication and of the dressing beyond necessity that characterizes the dandy.

The sanctioning of the dandy in the 1980s was so broad and compelling as to suggest the approach of a new *fin-de-siècle*. In his 1987–88 collections for men, Japanese designer Yohji Yamamoto emphasized the nineteenth-century heritage of the dandy in visions of slouchy jackets and loose foulards. In 1987, his fellow countrywoman Rei Kawakubo, of Comme des Garçons, also created a company of dandies, with an obsession for details, collars, and revisionist jackets seemingly unprecedented in mainstream fashion design for men. But the dandy styling is not only the prerogative of the designer; the dandy is, as always, self-created, as in the self-conscious poseur photographed by Josef Astor (1987), who creates a bewitching imagery that combines khakis with a double-breasted sports jacket and the loose gathering of a scarf at the neck. To be sure, pose reinforces the image, the type of the dandy suggesting a self-concerned and nonaggressive involution. The dancer Michael Clark, in a remarkable suite of poses conceived by Lord Snowdon in 1987, wears the attire of the dandy and creates the semblance vividly through his Hamlet-invoking contemplation, staged inquiry, eccentric coiffure, and the ceremony of the black cape. The return of lace for men, as in the collars and cuffs of his Comme des Garçons shirts, may seem aberrational, but its extreme form is only a version of the exacting requirements of men of distinction and prestige. His cape brings to mind associations with Charles Baudelaire, himself a nineteenth-century dandy. In *Paris Fashion* (1988), Valerie Steele refers to the "triumph of black—the cornerstone of Baudelaire's personal dandyism" as a bohemian black, defying the most respectable black and offering the dandy his personal synthesis of the Establishment and the renegade.

Conversely, the dandy also claims white, most especially the white suit, favored for example, by the American writer Mark Twain. The author of *Tom Sawyer* and *Huckleberry Finn* may have known the rural South, but he also knew the concept of the urban dandy and practiced the role in his personal presentation and performances, often with a kind of incipient theatricality. The dandy's white suit was easily commingled with that of the colonial and the adventurer. Theodore Roosevelt's white suit and the whiteness of his Panama hat (manifestly misnamed: the Panama is, of course, made in Ecuador) left a lasting impression on the American population through a 1906 photograph of the President wearing his *fino* at a construction site for the Panama Canal. Inexact in its geography, the Panama is nonetheless one of the most exacting hats to manufacture, requiring thin strips of jipijapa palm leaves woven while moist. Treasured and prestigious in the era of men's hats—in the late 1940s, the importing company Trans American Panama Hat Corporation sold 360,000 Panamas in one season—the Panama was also a favorite in Hollywood, where its wearers were as wily as Charlie Chan, as lugubrious as Sidney Greenstreet, and as suave as Alec Guinness.

The white suit kept its aesthetic purity throughout the first decades of the century, an era when servants were available for its cleaning. It also appealed to such Hollywood dandies as Humphrey Bogart, who wore it in tropical leisure. As worn by Robert Redford in the film of F. Scott Fitzgerald's *Great Gatsby* (1974), the white suit is another Hollywood triumph; its articulation of the vanity-prone male served per-

sts David McDermott and Pe-
McGough create a studied his-
cism in their art and their dress.
e determined archaism of their
e is a vision of the vintage dan-
an evocation of past dandyism,
ch exists beyond the superflui-
that classify other mortals.

*OSITE: David McDermott and Peter
Gough. 1987. Photographer: Marcus
therdale. Courtesy T. Greathouse
ery.*

Dandyism may be as nuanced as
the wearing of archaistic accessories or as exaggerated as the donning of an entire Henley-style outfit. Moreover, the dandy is the
creature of the big city: he thrives
in a society where he can be seen
in relief. He stands out as a visible
presence in a metropolis such as
London, Paris, Tokyo, or New
York.

*ABOVE: From left, Richard Merkin, Ed
Hayes, and Tom Wolfe. Published in*
Vanity Fair, *New York, October 1987.
Photographer: Neil Selkirk. © 1987
Neil Selkirk.*

The ability to wear a scarf with panache is the gift of the dandy. His is a swaddled narcissism of self-involvement and flamboyant expression.

OPPOSITE: Quentin Crisp. c. 1979. Photographer: Francesco Scavullo. Courtesy the photographer. LEFT: Orson Welles. 1979. Photographer: Timothy Greenfield-Sanders. © 1979 Timothy Greenfield-Sanders. BOTTOM LEFT: Jean Cocteau. 1937. Photographer: Jean Moral. Courtesy Staley-Wise Gallery.

Laconic in speech, dandies nevertheless devote themselves to an elaborate origami of nineteenth-century styles in tying the scarf, cravat, or neckpiece.

TOP: David McDermott. 1976. Photographer: Josef Astor. Courtesy the photographer. LEFT: Ensemble by Salvatore Ferragamo; cashmere blanket by Agnona. Published in L'Uomo Vogue, *Milan, July–August 1987. Photographer: Maria Vittoria Corradi. Courtesy Edizioni Conde Nast S.p.A.*

fectly the man of manifold shirts and sinister success. In 1974, show business stepped in where dandies of the arts refused to tread as the white suit's distinctiveness now became the mark not of poets but of playboys such as Hugh Hefner. The zenith and nadir of the white suit was achieved simultaneously in John Travolta's white-polyester-clad dervish in *Saturday Night Fever* (1977). Almost a decade passed from *Saturday Night Fever* to white's return to dandyism in the hands of the Italian designer Gianni Versace, who in 1985 altered it with the suggestion of leisure. But the supple drapery of the revised version sharply differentiated it from the polyester stiffness of the Travolta look, which had gathered momentum in the wake of his film, a movie that had a brief but intense impact on men's clothing and popular culture.

Another suit of dandy preference had a more profound impact on American culture, though it too walked the tightrope between respectability and the extreme. The zoot suit, which had been favored by blacks and Chicanos in the early 1940s, typically consisted of a knee-length coat with broad, square, padded shoulders and peg-top pants that ballooned at the knees and tapered to narrow cuffs. In 1943, as the Second World War was drawing to a close, the zoot-suit style, featuring an excess of material and oversizing that had been patriotically denied to the civilian population during the war, became extremely distasteful to some. Although *Newsweek* magazine in 1942 had informally—and perhaps approvingly—referred to it as the "drape shape," the zoot suit was also perceived as a protest against the war, its austerity, and its conformity. So savage was the reaction to this assumed disloyalty that men in zoot suits were beaten and stripped by those who found their garb objectionable. The continuing, though modified, allure of the style suggests not only its durability but its pertinence to the dandy, who disclaims the conservatism of most men's dress. It represents an ideal of adolescent rebellion: to enjoy the time of adulthood without its constraints, to live in an era of style exaggeration before all becomes sublimated and suborned. Like the dandy's continuing association with the hip and hipsters, his attachment to the zoot style emanates from his

The external lassitude of the dandy, a study in world-weary indifference, is not, of course, incompatible with his expenditure of energies in narcissism and self-avowal.

ABOVE: Fashion editor Hamish Bowles wearing blazer, shirt, pants, and scarf by Aquascutum; overcoat by Aquascutum at Old England; shoes by Hackett. Fashion editorial published in Vogue Hommes, *Paris, March 1987. Photographer: Lord Snowdon. Courtesy Editions Condé Nast S.A. OPPOSITE: Jacket and shirt by Compagnia delle Pelli; scarf by Charvet; boots by Blackstone for Petris. Published in* Per Lui, *Milan, July–August 1987. Photographer: William Laxton.*

Le Comte Robert de Montes-quiou-Fezensec, dandy paradigm of the *fin de siècle* in pearl-gray suit, great cravat, and walking stick, was a poet and essayist and himself the literary source for dandies depicted by Marcel Proust and Joris Karl Huysmans. A famous account claimed that Montesquiou, caught one evening in a nightclub fire, used his cane to bludgeon women and children in his way so that he could be the first to escape. Although the story is false and even libelous, it points up the dandy's critical dilemma in his acceptance of the role: is his moral responsibility to himself or to others? Polonius's advice—"to thine own self be true"—notwithstanding, the dandy is condemned by some for narcissism exceeding social responsibility.

ABOVE: Le Comte Robert de Montesquiou. *1897. Painting by Giovanni Boldini. Collection Réunion des Musées Nationaux, Musée d'Orsay, Paris.*

In his dress as in his art and his collections, fashion designer Karl Lagerfeld returned to the past for inspiration in the 1970s. His wing collar is complemented by an anachronistic monocle.

LEFT: Karl Lagerfeld. 1974. Photographer: Helmut Newton. Courtesy the photographer.

A man reading a menswear journal just after the turn of the century wears an elevated collar suggestive of a waning era.

ABOVE: Twentieth-century gentleman. c. 1905. Unknown photographer. Courtesy Library of Congress.

Throwing caution to the winds, Karl Lagerfeld moves from wing collar to high collar, and *le tout Paris* is at his feet.

LEFT: Karl Lagerfeld. 1976. Photographer: Helmut Newton. Courtesy the photographer.

High and doubled collars frame the face, defying modern conventions of male dress.

ABOVE: Arto Lindsey. 1986. Photographer: Josef Astor. Courtesy the photographer.

oubled collar, Edwardian bow,
assertive jacket with giant,
versation-provoking buttons
rays the sheepish isolation of
contemporary dandy placed in
tting of geometric and theatri-
artifice.

VE: *Fashion portrait. 1987. Adver-*
nent. Photographer: Josef Astor.
rtesy the photographer.

In a suite of portraits, dancer-choreographer Michael Clark interprets the dandy with Hamletlike contemplativeness, distinct reserve, and aesthetic beauty. Clark abets the aesthetic with a contrived coiffure in the manner of Aubrey Beardsley.

ABOVE: *Michael Clark in cashmere cape by Nikos; shirt by Comme des Garçons.* OPPOSITE TOP: *Michael Clark, with model. Ensembles by Mario Valentino; shirts by Richard Cornejo.* OPPOSITE BOTTOM: *Michael Clark wearing jacket by Nikos; lounging coat by Jean Muir; shirt by Comme des Garçons. Fashion editorial published in* L'Uomo Vogue, *Milan,*

December 1987. Photographer: L Snowdon. Courtesy Edizioni Conde S.p.A.

In the mid-1980s bows appeared in
the refurbished Edwardian suits of
Comme des Garçons.

*ABOVE: Ensemble by Comme des Garçons;
hat by Bernstock & Speirs. Fashion editorial published in* Vogue Hommes International, *Paris, Spring–Summer
1988. Photographer: Michael Wooley.
Courtesy Publications Condé Nast S.A.*

The white suit is the sartorial equivalent of the white whale. The emblem of innocence and purity, it is the embodiment of clothing without human concession. Descriptively, it defies the possibilities of dirt and heat in warm weather; metaphorically, it is a triumph of the dandy over his environment, suffering neither grime nor compromise.

LEFT: Samuel Clemens (Mark Twain). c. 1900. Unknown photographer. Courtesy Library of Congress. BOTTOM LEFT: President Theodore Roosevelt running an American steam shovel at Culebra Cut, Panama Canal. 1906. Photographer: Underwood and Underwood from a stereoscopic view. Courtesy New-York Historical Society.

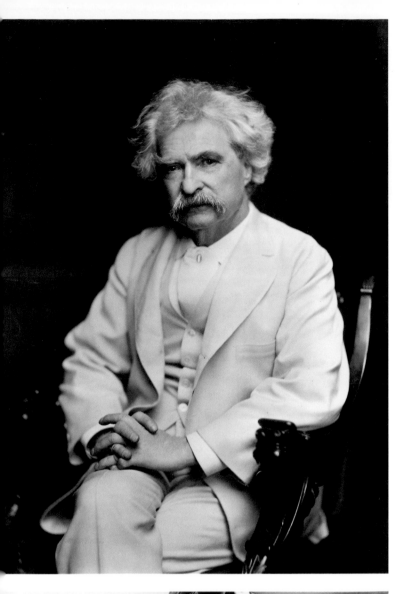

A romantic figure in an exotic locale, the hero in white suit brings elegance to the lushness of Southern California.

ABOVE: Humphrey Bogart. c. 1942. Unknown photographer for Warner Bros.-Vitaphone Pictures. Courtesy Kobal Collection.

The mirrored narcissism of the dandy, visualized in a 1974 film about the parvenu Jay Gatsby, was given further expression in an elaborate Ralph Lauren wardrobe that included a white, three-piece suit. British rock-video producer, disk jockey, and musician Don Letts, opposite, once said: "I sort of flit between two different styles, Sambo First Blood Claat and Our Man in Havana," the latter preference evident in his selection of a white suit.

LEFT: Robert Redford in The Great Gatsby. *1974. Unknown photographer for Paramount Pictures. Courtesy Kobal Collection. OPPOSITE: Don Letts. 1987. Published in* Arena, London, July– *August 1987. Photographer: Eamon J. McCabe. Courtesy the photographer.*

The polyester white suit epitomizes the inescapable circumstances of Brooklyn disco life in the film *Saturday Night Fever* (1977). What had been the most select item of the dandy's wardrobe became jejune and garish in its new fabric and milieu.

ABOVE LEFT: John Travolta in Saturday Night Fever. *1977. Unknown photographer for Paramount Pictures. Courtesy Kobal Collection. ABOVE RIGHT: Hugh Hefner and Playboy Bunnies. c. 1975. Unknown photographer. Courtesy Bettmann Archive.*

n in white evoke sacred and
ing vocations, as well as the
of tropical nights. The range
ese evocations suggests that
te garb is not ordinary but rath-
xtraordinary and uplifting.

_SITE: Advertisement for Gianni
ace. Published in_ Vogue Hommes,
_, April 1985. Photographer: Claus
rath. Courtesy Gianni Versace._

Radical at its inception in the
1930s, the zoot suit underwent a
rapid diffusion. Although it ex-
cited street violence in the 1940s,
it was appropriated by smart urban
youth; it hit the suburbs a decade
later, under the banner of rock and
roll and the gentle force of fashion's accommodation of radical
gesture to dandy styles. In the
1980s, zoot followed suit in the
general historical revival of past
styles. The exaggerated proportions of the large jacket and severe-
ly pegged pants are underscored by
the violent patterning.

TOP LEFT: Zoot suit. 1942. Published in
Life, _September 21, 1942. Photographer:
Marie Hansen. Courtesy Time Inc. CEN-
TER LEFT: Savoy Ballroom, Harlem.
Late 1930s. Unknown photographer.
Courtesy Bettmann Archive. BOTTOM
LEFT: Mount Vernon High School,
Alexandria, Virginia. 1957. Unknown
photographer. Courtesy Smithsonian In-
stitution. ABOVE: Anthony in tartan suit.
Fashion editorial published in_ L'Uomo
Vogue, _Milan, December 1981. Photog-
rapher: Amy Arbus. © 1981 Amy Arbus._

As if the full pants of the zoot suit had collapsed into an overskirt, the trousers in the design by Frenchman Jean-Paul Gaultier in 1985 had an overdrape across the front that formed their own apron. Earlier, in a 1978 collection, British designer Vivienne Westwood had showed men's suits with overskirts over narrow trousers, and in 1988, had shown kilted suits; in 1983,

American designer Stephen Sprouse would have a male model walk down the runway at a showing of his collection with a black denim miniskirt over black jeans.

ABOVE: Suit with skirt-pants by Jean-Paul Gaultier. Published in Vogue Hommes International, *Paris, Spring–Summer 1985. Courtesy Publications Condé Nast S.A.*

In a 1980s zoot suit with frock-coat-length jacket, high-waisted pegged trousers, open 1940s collar, and pin striping, the traditional zoot elegance and radicalism are reassembled by a new generation.

OPPOSITE: Chris Sullivan in zoot suit. Fashion editorial published in L'Uomo Vogue, *Milan, December 1981. Photographer: Tony McGee. Courtesy Edizioni Conde Nast S.p.A.*

sense of the visible chic of rebellion/style differentiation. One of the most dandyesque of the contemporary European designers, Jean-Paul Gaultier, designed a 1985 zoot suit with a pin-striped jacket and the accoutrements of oversized tie, long watch chain, and showy cuffs, all harking back to the zoot suit at its most defiant, while adding a completely contemporary touch of a skirt to the trousers. As a fashion concept, the zoot suit is all but inevitable: there must be an ironic and extreme form of the suit that can be used to call the pervasive conventionality of the garment into question.

The suit extremes reflected in the zoot style of the 1940s and 1980s also found other expressions, as in the Pierre Cardin collarless suits adopted by the Beatles in the 1960s. The early style role of these young dandies was unquestionably a significant factor in bringing worldwide attention to a Britain whose Empire was in decline. The Beatles were initially found controversial; their haircuts and suits signified radical change, and their defiance of convention was thought to be as fearsome as that of the zoot-suit wearers a quarter of a century earlier. Nevertheless, the sartorial assertion of the Beatles permitted a sartorial explosion along London's Carnaby Street and its production of Mod clothing styles in the mid-1960s; there emerged a dandyism that betrayed its radicalism by constant references to the past. Waistcoats, paisley and floral patterns, boaters, high-rise collars, wide belts, and bell-bottom trousers all were ushered in via the dandy. The Beatles themselves followed a sartorial spiral, soon discarding ties (the Nehru jacket followed in 1966), and reached an apogee of theatricality in the colorful satin uniforms trimmed with braid worn on the cover of *Sergeant Pepper's Lonely Hearts Club Band* (1967). This marked a turning point in the Mod options offered in Great Britain, France, and America; initially liberated by the Beatles, the 1960s dandy was moving onward to velvet suits, high-heeled shoes, ethnic dress, animal patterns, and jewelry in a transformation known as the Peacock Revolution.

What that revolution permitted was a critical review of the history of Western dress, the opportunity to incorporate into it ideas and forms from outside the canon of Western costume, and the social liberation of the man to exist beyond certain conventions of colors, styles, and habits. Sexual liberation and individual liberties moved in tandem with freedom of dress and supported similar goals. The Peacock Revolution was, however, an episode and not an epoch. Although some of its dandies remain (it was a prime period for such traditional artistic dandies as Salvador Dali), it has had little persistence or long-range impact. It occasioned the dandyism of Superfly and sparked other extravagant black styles of dress, but few of these have retained the importance of the zoot suit. Ethnic and theatrical embellishment were vividly flaunted by such celebrities as Roger Daltry of the Who as late as 1975, when the rock-opera *Tommy* appeared on film. But it was the final, high tide of the Peacock Revolution before the dynamics of the freedom and dandyism of the Beatles ebbed away in a cruel assassination off New York's Central Park West in 1980.

Ever are there dandies, for their style is without time. The dandy has his own special conviction; he challenges all style yet strives to be a new style, at least unto himself. The dynamic of the dandy and his perseverance through the twentieth century testifies to style's flexibility and magnitude.

The young English rock group that called itself the Beatles helped generate the youthful style movement that overtook the 1960s. The reductive modernism of the group's Pierre Cardin suits without lapels defied the conventions of Savile Row, the bastion of British tailoring.

ABOVE: *The Beatles. c. 1963. Unknown photographer. Courtesy Michael Ochs Archive.*

The Mod style of the early 1960s was replaced by a new set of historical references later in the decade—the Edwardian revival, the baroque haberdashery inspired by the Beatles's cover for *Sergeant Pepper's Lonely Hearts Club Band* (1967), and the rock group's own florid revivalism on the *Abbey Road* cover (1969). By the time the Beatles paraded across Abbey Road, the 1970s were at hand—in its style individuation and in the jeans, dishevelment, and hirsuteness of George Harrison.

ABOVE: The Beatles in the cover image for their album Abbey Road. *1969. Photographer: Iain Macmillan. Courtesy Magnum Photos, Inc. TOP RIGHT: Beatles fans in London. Published in* Life, *New York, January 31, 1964. Photographer: Terence Spencer. Courtesy the photographer. CENTER RIGHT: Carnaby Street. Published in* Life, *May 13, 1966. Photographer: Terence Spencer. Courtesy Time Inc. BOTTOM: Chicago students in Mod dress. Cover of* Life, *May 13, 1966. Photographer: Henry Grossman. Courtesy Time Inc.*

BACK IN THE GROOVE

Even those styles of the 1960s th
were endemic to the specific poli
cal and social circumstances of th
time have been reassimilated by
men's style in the 1980s.

*FAR LEFT: Ensemble by Franco Mosca
no. Fashion editorial published in mea
edition of* Italian Design Fashio
*Florence, 1988–89. Photographer: Pie
Schwab. Courtesy Toscoeditrice. LEI
1960s revival. Fashion editorial pu
lished in* Life, *August 1985. Photogr
pher: Tony Costa. Courtesy Time I
OPPOSITE: Jacket by Massimo Osti j
C.P. Collection; shirt by Paul Smith; t
by Liberty of London; tie by Emilio Puc
shoes by Alan MacAfee. Published in P
Lui, Milan, October 1987. Photogr
pher: Mario Testino. Courtesy Edizic
Conde Nast S.p.A.*

At the end of the 1960s, hippies introduced colorful assemblages of
craft work, second-hand clothing,
and ethnic dress to menswear. Although business executives would
not wear beads to the office, the
former Harvard professor Timothy
Leary and other "drop-outs" gave
up clothing conventions for hand-
work gestures; other men took to
wearing weekend jewelry, adorn-
ing themselves on their days off
with multiple chains at neck and
chest, bracelets, macramé, and
other craft accessories.

ABOVE: Hippies. Published in Horizon,
*New York, 1968. Photographer: Don
Snyder. Courtesy the photographer.*

Dandies of all generations were
freed in the 1970s to take on the
stripes of an endangered species

*FOLLOWING PAGES, LEFT: Salva
Dali, Hotel Meurice, Paris. 1973. I
tographer: Helmut Newton. Courtesy
photographer. RIGHT: Patrice Calme
1970. Photographer: Francesco Scav
Courtesy the photographer.*

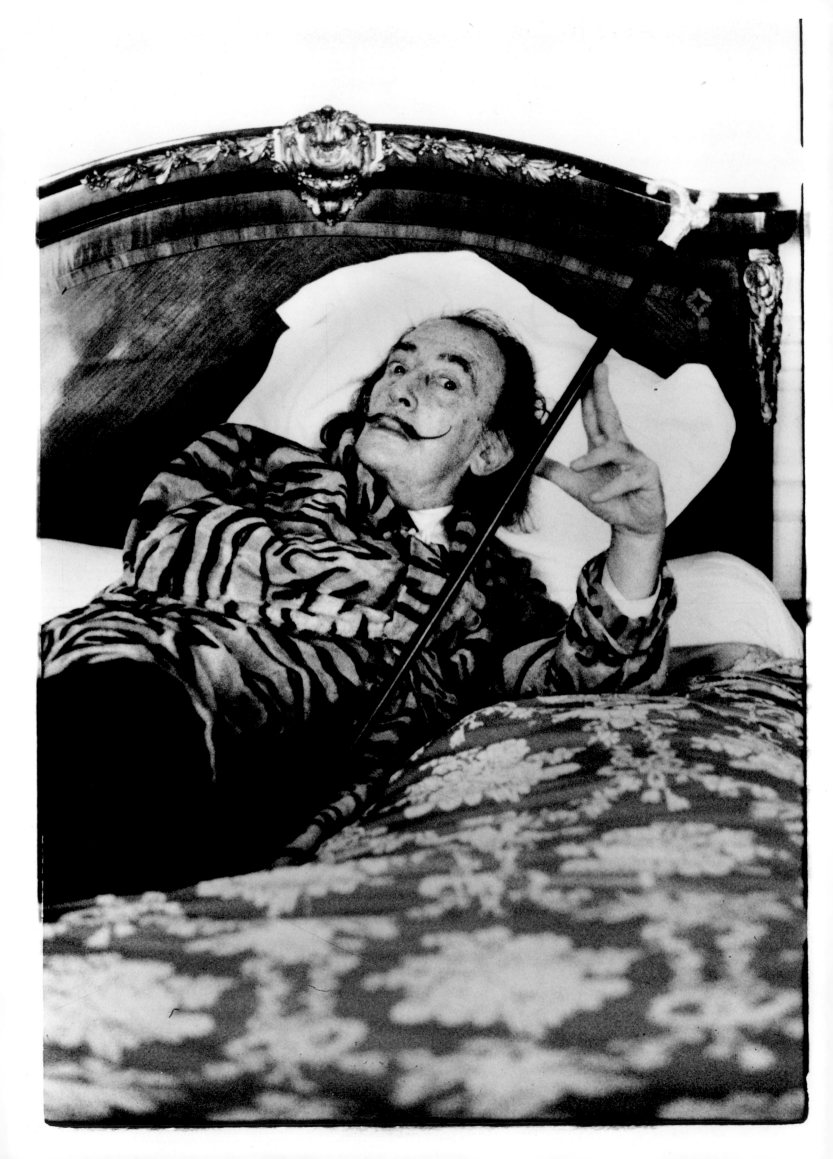

Theatrical clothing that evolved from the "Peacock Revolution" entered into many arenas, most especially the spectatorship of Muhammad Ali fans. Known as Ali's Army, they dressed not for conformity but for the ostentatious display of wealth and the good time it buys for the dandy.

OPPOSITE: Spectator at the Muhammad Ali–Oscar Bonavena boxing match, Madison Square Garden, New York. Published in Life, *December 18, 1970. Photographer: Dominique Berretty for Keystone. Courtesy Time Inc.*

Dandies plundered not only their Western heritage but also the sumptuous possibilities of North Africa and the East. As men sought to be more expressive in the late 1960s and 1970s, they found a logical correlation with non-Western clothing.

ABOVE LEFT: Greek actor Takis Emmanuel wearing a Moroccan caftan. Fashion editorial published in Life, *September 25, 1970. Photographer: Enrico Sarsini. Courtesy the photographer. ABOVE RIGHT: Patrick Lichfield. Published in* Life, *July 26, 1968. Photographer: Loomis Dean. Courtesy Time Inc.*

o designers bring underage chic
over-sized zoot suits and fey
icism to the role of the dandy.

*OSITE: Devon and Hiro wearing suits
l hats by Mitso for Akafuji; shirts and
ssories by Richard Utilla. Fashion
torial published in i-D, London,
rch 1986. Photographer: Isabel Sny-
Courtesy the photographer.*

BIBLIOGRAPHY

The literature on men's clothing and style is found in many places. Men's fashion magazines—such as *Esquire*, *GQ*, *M*, and *Daily News Record* in the United States; *Mondo Uomo*, *Per Lui*, *Uomo Collezioni*, *Uomo Harper's Bazaar*, *L'Uomo Vogue*, and *Vanity* in Italy; *L'Officiel Hommes*, *Vogue Hommes*, and *Vogue Hommes International* in France; *Vogue Manner* in Germany; *Arena* in England; *Otoko* and *Men's Club* in Japan; and *Follow Me, Gentlemen* in Australia—have created a substantial body of literature that has been excluded from this bibliography owing to its sheer quantity. Earlier journals—especially *Adam* (Paris, 1924–52), *Gentry* (New York, 1951–57), and *Sartorial Art Journal* (London, 1874–1929)—provide additional insights into the subject of men's clothing.

Adams, Laverne S. "The Shopping Behavior of Men in Purchasing Suits." Master's thesis, Mankato State College, 1971.

Baker, Carlos. *Ernest Hemingway: A Life Story*. New York, 1969.

Baker, Russell. "Smelling Like a New Man," *The New York Times*, December 2, 1965.

Barney, Sydney. *Clothes and the Man*. London, 1951.

Baudelaire, Charles. *The Painter of Modern Life and Other Essays*. Translated by Jonathan Mayne. London, 1964.

Bennett-England, Rodney. *Dress Optional: The Revolution in Menswear*. London, 1967.

Binder, Pearl. *The Peacock's Tail*. London, 1958.

Boyer, G. Bruce. *Elegance: A Guide to Quality in Menswear*. New York, 1985.

Brooks, John. "Beyond the Man in the Gray Flannel Suit," *The New York Times Magazine*, April 17, 1977.

Brubach, Holly. "Men will be Men," *The Atlantic Monthly*, April 1983.

Bull, Bartle. *Safari: A Chronicle of Adventure*. New York, 1988.

Burman, Barbara, and Melissa Leventon. "The Men's Dress Reform Party, 1929–37," *Costume*, 1987.

Byrde, Penelope. *The Male Image: Men's Fashion in Britain, 1300–1970*. London, 1979.

Carlsen, Peter, and William Wilson. *Manstyle: The GQ Guide to Fashion, Fitness, and Grooming*. New York, 1977.

Carlyle, Thomas. *Sartor Resartus*. London, 1908.

Coleman, Elizabeth Ann. *Of Men Only: A Review of Men's and Boys' Fashions, 1750–1975*, Brooklyn, New York, 1975.

Cobrin, Harry A. *The Men's Clothing Industry: Colonial through Modern Times*. New York, 1970.

"Courting the Clothes Hound," *Newsweek*, October 3, 1983.

Cunnington, C. W. and Phillis. *A Handbook of English Costume in the Nineteenth Century*. Boston, 1970.

Cunnington, Phillis, and Ann Mansfield. *A Handbook of English Costume in the Twentieth Century*. Boston, 1973.

Dary, David. *Cowboy Culture: A Saga of Five Centuries*. New York, 1981.

Dichter, Ernest. "Peacock Revolution," *American Fabrics and Fashions* 71, 1966.

Disfarmer: The Heber Springs Portraits, 1939–1946. 1976.

Doke, Donald. *The Consumer's Guide to Menswear*. New York, 1983.

Dorsey, Hebe. "The Enduring Appeal of Pinstripes," *The Institutional Investor*, December 1982.

Duka, John. "Skirts for Men? Yes and No," *The New York Times*, October 27, 1984.

Dyer, Rod, and Ron Spark. *Fit to Be Tied: Vintage Ties of the Forties and Early Fifties*. New York, 1987.

Easthope, Antony. *What a Man's Gotta Do: The Masculine Myth in Popular Culture*, London, 1986.

Ehrenreich, Barbara. *The Hearts of Men*. New York, 1983.

Farren, Mick. *The Black Leather Jacket*. New York, 1985.

Fenin, George H., and William K. Everson. *The Western: From Silents to Cinerama*. New York, 1962.

Fields, Mike, with contributions by A. Peter Bailey. *Getting It Together: The Black Man's Guide to Good Grooming and Fashion*. New York, 1983.

Flusser, Alan. *Clothes and the Man*. New York, 1988.

——— . *Making the Man*. New York, 1981.

Franklin, Clyde W. *The Changing Definition of Masculinity*. New York, 1984.

Furstenberg, Egon von, with Camille Duhe. *The Power Look*. New York, 1978.

Gale, William, and the editors of *Esquire*. *Esquire's Fashions for Today*. New York. 1973.

Gingold, Alfred. "Hey Dude," *New York Woman*, September 1987.

Gleichen-Russwurm, Alexander von. *Dandies and Don Juans: Concerning Fashion and Love among the Great*. New York, 1928.

Green, Martin Burgess. *Children of the Sun: A Narrative of "Decadence" in England after 1918*. New York, 1976.

Hawes, Elizabeth. *Men Can Take It*. New York, 1939.

"History of the Men's Wear Industry, 1890–1950," *Men's Wear*, February 10, 1950 [special issue].

Hix, Charles. *Dressing Right*. New York, 1978.

——— . *How to Dress Your Man*. New York, 1981.

——— . *Looking Good*. New York, 1977.

——— . *Man Alive!* New York, 1984.

Juster, Harry. *Clothes Make the Man*. New York, 1965.

ashima, Masaaki. *Fundamentals of Men's Fashion Design.* New York, 5.

ffmann, Sandra. *The Cowboy Catalog.* New York, 1980.

rs, Paul. *A Gentleman's Wardrobe.* New York, 1987.

:hel, Walter, III. "The Managerial Dress Code," *Fortune,* April 4, 3.

n, Edward, and Don Erickson, eds. *About Men: Reflections on the ? Experience.* New York, 1987.

da, Michael. *Male Chauvinism!: How It Works.* New York, 1973.

itt, Mortimer. *The Executive Look.* New York, 1983.

ie, Alison. *The Language of Clothes.* New York, 1981.

de Plumage '68," *Newsweek,* November 25, 1968.

Marley, Diana. *Fashion for Men.* New York, 1985.

tin, Richard. "The Function of Fashion in Baudelaire's 'Le Peintre a vie moderne' (1863)," *Dress,* 1984.

——— . "Post-Modern Menswear: Irony and Anomaly in Men's Attire he 1980s," *Dress,* 1982.

Gill, Leonard. *Stylewise.* New York, 1983.

Quade, William. "High Style Disrupts the Men's Wear Industry," une, February 1971.

ard, Lawrence. "Executive Suit," *Forbes,* May 24, 1982.

rs, Ellen. *The Dandy: Brummell to Beerbohn.* London, 1960.

loy, John T. *Dress for Success.* New York, 1975.

son, Sara. "The Male Market Defined with a Capital M," *Advertis-lge,* September 5, 1983.

ourke, P. J. "WASPish Hats Lend Themselves to Madcap Follies," ' *Street Journal.*

etti, Jo Barraclough. "Ridicule and Role Models as Factors in Amer-Men's Fashion Change, 1880–1910," *Costume,* 1985.

k, J. H., and E. H. Pleck. *The American Man.* Englewood Cliffs, Jersey, 1980.

, Henry. *The Ultimate Man.* New York, 1978.

:, H. P. *When Men Wore Muffs.* London, 1936.

ardson, Michael. "Outback Couture: Riding High on the 'Crocodile dee' Look," *International Herald Tribune,* July 21, 1987.

Riesman, David. *Individualism Reconsidered and Other Essays.* Glencoe, Illinois, 1954.

Rolo, Charles J. "A Man's Guide to Dressing Well for Business," *Money,* February 1982.

Savage, William W. *The Cowboy Hero: His Image in American History and Culture.* Norman, Oklahoma, 1979.

Schoeffler, O. E., and William Gale. *Esquire's Encyclopedia of 20th Century Men's Fashion.* New York, 1973.

"Seventy-five Years of Fashion: A Pictorial Review of Men's Fashions and Fashion Influences," *Men's Wear,* June 25, 1965 [special issue].

Shaw, William Harlan. *American Men's Wear, 1861–1982.* Baton Rouge, Louisiana, 1982.

Solomon, Michael Robert. "Dress for Success: Clothing Appropriations and the Efficacy of Role Behavior." Ph.D. thesis, University of North Carolina at Chapel Hill, 1981.

Sprague, Marshall. *A Gallery of Dudes.* Boston, 1966.

Steele, H. Thomas. *The Hawaiian Shirt: Its Art and History.* New York, 1984.

Stote, Dorothy. *Men Too Wear Clothes.* New York, 1939.

Strycker, Roy E., and Nancy Wood. *In This Proud Land: America 1935–1943 as Seen in the FSA Photographs.* Greenwich, Connecticut, 1973.

Sweeting, C. G. *Combat Flying Clothing.* Washington, D.C., 1984.

Tiger, Lionel. *Men in Groups.* New York, 1969.

Trachtenberg, Jeffrey A. "Executive Suit," *Forbes,* March 26, 1984.

Weiner, Steve. "Trench Coats Have Pizazz and Mystique But May Be All Wet," *Wall Street Journal,* October 1984.

Weitz, John. *Man in Charge: The Executive's Guide to Grooming, Manners, Travel.* New York, 1974.

Wilson, Sloan. *The Man in the Gray Flannel Suit.* New York, 1955.

——— . *What Shall We Wear to This Party? The Man in the Gray Flannel Suit Twenty Years Before & After.* New York, 1976.

Wilson, William, and the editors of *Esquire. Man at His Best: The Esquire Guide to Style.* Reading, Massachusetts, 1985.

"You're So Vain" (special section), *Newsweek,* April 14, 1986.

ACKNOWLEDGMENTS

Men's style is not only recorded by gifted photographers, it is created by them. We are grateful to Bob Adelman, Ted Allan, Thomas Anders, Amy Arbus, Eve Arnold, Josef Astor, Richard Avedon, Jeannette Barron, Cecil Beaton, Gilles Bensimon, Antoni Bernad, Koto Bolofo, Hugh Brown, Buffalo (Ray Petrie and Jamie Morgan), Robert Capa, Henri Cartier-Bresson, Alex Chatelain, George Chinsee, Maria Vittoria Corradi, Tony Costa, Dan Coxe, J. Cowley, Gerry Cranham, Imogen Cunningham, Loomis Dean, François Deconinck, Jean-Philippe Decros, Michael Disfarmer, Alfred Eisenstaedt, Arthur Elgort, John Engstead, Jon Ericson, Elliott Erwitt, Michael Evans, Aldo Fallai, Hymie Fink, Jill Freedman, Victoria Gewirz, Gerry Goodstein, Greg Gorman, Peter Gravelle, Timothy Greenfield-Sanders, Ken Griffiths, André Grossman, Romano Grozic, Yoni Hamenachem, Pamela Hanson, Charles Harbutt, Thurston Hopkins, Kevin Horan, Horst P. Horst, George Hoyningen-Huene, David Hurn, George Hurrell, Claude Jaques, Tim Jenkins, Yale Joel, Philip Kamin, Yousuf Karsh, Nick Knight, Kim Knott, Mark Kozlowski, Bob Krieger, Xavier Lambours, William Laxton, Marcus Leatherdale, Russell Lee, Patrick Lichfield, Marcia Lippman, Adelle Lutz, Danny Lyon, Joan Marcus, Mary Ellen Mark, Kurt Markus, Wayne Maser, Tom McBride, Eamonn J. McCabe, Tony McGee, Barry McKinley, Keith McManus, Andrew McPherson, Amy Meadow, Steven Meisel, Giordano Morganti, Noboru Morikawa, Claude Mougin, Nadir, Monte Nagler, Helmut Newton, Perry Ogden, Scott Osman, A. Y. Owen, Richard Pandiscio, Rondal Partridge, Hy Peskin, Barney Peterson, E.R. Richee, Arthur Rickerby, Herb Ritts, Michael Roberts, Zade Rosenthal, Enrico Sarsini, Francesco Scavullo, Paul Schutzer, Pierre Schwab, Nick Scott, Neil Selkirk, Ellen Shanley, W. Eugene Smith, The Earl of Snowdon, Dan Snyder, Isabel Snyder, Terence Spencer, Lance Staedler, Edward Steichen, Dennis Stock, Bico Stupakoff, Tony Thorimbert, Mario Testino, Steve Tynan, Burk Uzzle, Frédérique Veysset, Raymond Voinquel, Barbra Walz, Albert Watson, Dan Weaks, Dan Weiner, Theo Westenburger, Claus Wickrath, Laszlo Willinger, Leroy Woodson, Michael Wooley, and Peter Zander.

Heroes in kindness include Woody Allen, Jeffrey Banks, David Byrne, Art Carney, Pee-wee Herman, Quincy Jones, Arnold Palmer, Charles Roman, Michael Schau, Arnold Schwarzenegger, and Bobby Short.

We are also grateful to Kathryn Abbe; Addison Gallery of American Art, Phillips Academy, Andover, Massachusetts, Nicki Thiras; Agence Vu, Sophie; Ally and Gargano, Tom Stenovec; *Arena*, Chris Logan; Marc Ascoli; Bettmann Archive, Peter Dervis; Big City Productions, Gary Hurewitz; Bloomingdale's, John Jay; Dan Brennan; Camel Cigarettes / R. J. Reynolds Tobacco, U.S.A., Jo Spach; Woodfin Camp; Chaz / Revlon, Inc., George Field; Columbia Pictures, Iva Orta; Comme des Garçons, Marion Greenberg and Lauren Hanna; Condé Nast International, Melanie Kang; Conde Nast Italia, Milli Gualteroni: The Condé Nast Publications, Inc., Diana Edkins; Corneliani, Mrs. Valeria; Delaney Fletcher Delaney, Tom Knox; Christian Dior, Gloria McPike; Elgort studio, Ronit Auneri; *Esquire* Magazine, Jayne Hendel; The Gap, Maggie Gross and Shelly Wargo; Greg Gorman Studio, Rob Platz; T. Greathouse

Gallery, Tim Greathouse; Yvonne Halsman; *Harper's Bazaar Uomo*, M Cavaglia; Harris & Goldberg Talent Agency, Rebecca Taylor; Hartmarx C poration, Frank Brenner; Harvard Theatre Collection, Pusey-Weidner brary, Harvard University, Cambridge, Massachusetts, Jeanne Newlin; H studio, Rick Tardiff; Mariana Houtenbos; International Museum of Phot raphy at George Eastman House, Rochester, New York, Barbara Galassi; *L ian Design Fashion*, Romano Carotti; JGK, Pam; Keeble Cavaco & Duka, Filipowski; Calvin Klein Industries, Paul Wilmot; Kobal Collection, E Cosenza; Eileen Lerner; Levi Strauss & Co., Dean Christon and Peggy J Little, Brown and Co., Jill O'Connell; Magnum Photos, Elizabeth Gallin Magazine, Fairchild Publications, Anita Bethel; Georges Marciano, Gues Inc., Lisa Hickey; Marlboro Cigarettes, Philip Morris & Co., Nancy Lu The Metropolitan Museum of Art Photograph and Slide Library, Mary D erty; Martine Mollard Agency, Françoise Bornstein; *Mondo Uomo*, Luise Montinengo; Franco Moschino; The Museum of Modern Art, New York, M Corliss, Susan Kismaric, Charles Silver; The Oakland Museum, Oakla California, Katherine Chambers; Michael Ochs Archives, Lynne Richards Ogilvy & Mather, Dan Levi; Overland Productions, Andrea Starr; Overs *Paper* Publishing Co., Kim Hastreiter and Maggie McCormick; Paris *Pass* Robert Sarner; Dan Passman, Esq.; *People* Magazine, Jody Mastronardi; M cuse Pfeifer Gallery, Marcuse Pfeifer; Réunion des Musées Nationaux, Pa Béatrice de Boisseson; Rizzoli, Bill Dworkin, Eve Gromek, Erika Lepi Mara Lurie; Rose's Lime Juice (Cadbury-Schweppes); San Francisco *Chron* Jody Carpenter; Barbara Schlager; Jillian Slonim; Sotheby's, London, Ly Cullen; *Sports Illustrated*, Mike Dixon; Studio Immagine, Beatrice Truck Time, Inc., Debra Cohen; Tri-Star Pictures; Twentieth Century Fox, Sh Klamer, Pat Miller; TWBA Advertising, Inc., Page Murray; Universal I tures, Nancy Cushing-Jones; Gianni Versace, Emanuela Schmeidler; Viaco Lynn Fero and Roseann Piliero; *The Village Voice*, Mim Ydovitch; *Vogue Homr* Jean Goussebaire; Voinquel studio, Pascal Legrand; Watson studio, A Kirkbride, Elisabeth Watson; Sandra Wiener; Wheeler Pictures, Elizab Sinsabaugh; The White House Photo Office, Carol McKay; Wisconsin Cer for Film and Theater Research, Maxine Fleckner Ducey; Witkin Gallery

At the Fashion Institute of Technology, Barbara Castle, Dorothy Rud Ellen Shanley, Irving Solero, and Tomoko Wheaton have made patient, nificant, and splendid contributions to this book. Etheleen Staley and T Wise of Staley-Wise Gallery have been as generous with ideas as with imag At Rizzoli, Charles Davey has been more than a designer and earned role his own: friend, counselor, advocate, critic, and pilot. But two women dese mention/*menschen* as they stand behind our echelon of men in roles. J Fluegel, at Rizzoli, as always, our Virgil as we ascend out of the circle our confusion; and Laura Sinderbrand, at the Fashion Institute of Techi ogy, is our triplet; her ideas are very much present in all that is seen and ir that might be envisioned by these two men.

RM and